UNIVERSAL DESIGN FOR LEARNING

A Guide for Teachers and Education Professionals

Council for Exceptional Children

The voice and vision of special education

PEARSON

Custom Publishing

PEARSON

Merrill Prentice Hall

Printed in the United States of America

10   9

ISBN 0-13-170160-6

2004220162

EH

The Council for Exceptional Children
1110 N. Glebe Road, Suite 300
Arlington, VA 22201-5704
Voice: 703/620-3660
TTY: 703/264-9446
Fax: 703/264-9494
www.cec.sped.org

PREFACE

Universal Design for Learning: A Guide for Teachers and Education Professionals is written for instructors in education classes as a means of informing current and future teachers about the basics of universal design for learning (UDL) and the ways it can be implemented in schools and classrooms.

The goal of this publication is to inform teachers of the basis for effective teaching practice and to remind them of the various instructional resources available for them to create a UDL environment in their own classrooms. It is worth noting an informed, dedicated teacher is the most essential factor in the success of UDL or any reform. Without a good teacher, the best methods and materials are, at best, ineffective.

Each chapter presents key questions and a scenario of the issues confronting educators for integrating universal design for learning concepts and strategies into the curriculum. After the Introduction, Chapter 1, "*Universal Design for Learning in Today's Diverse Schools,*" discusses how to think about curriculum design and instruction by exploring the links among UDL, assistive technology (AT) , and effective teaching. Chapter 2, "*Federal Legislation Supporting Universal Design for Learning and Assistive Technology,*" offers a brief history and review of the legal and ethical issues surrounding universal design for learning. Chapter 3, "*Instructional Theories Supporting Universal Design for Learning: Teaching to Individual Learners,*" discusses instructional theories that are fundamental to UDL. Chapter 4, "*Assistive Technology and Universal Design for Learning in Content Areas,*" provides available resources and technologies to successfully integrate AT into a UDL environment. Chapter 5, "*Collaborative Strategies for Universal Design for Learning Success,*" provides information on how to collaborate for success in a UDL environment. Throughout the guide, references and resources on professional growth for preservice and inservice teachers, as well as useful Web sites, are available on these topics.

The information in this text is intended to serve as a guide introducing the concept of universal design for learning to educators preparing to teach and those currently instructing students with disabilities. While the chapters are closely linked, instructors will find that several chapters can be used as stand-alone instructional units. These materials were designed specifically for use with general and special education courses on curriculum and methods, technology, and assistive technology. These materials are intended to supplement, not to supplant, regular course materials. To best facilitate understanding of how UDL relates to instructional components described in this text, instructors and learners should actively read with the intent of understanding:

- how UDL combined with instructional and assistive technologies and different learning theories can improve classroom instruction and student outcomes, and

- how curriculum/instruction would differ if UDL were embedded into materials, expectations, and classroom lessons.

The bulk of the text that follows has been drawn from current research and print-based resources, for two reasons: to demonstrate the extent of readily available information on universal design for learning and to provide an easy means for interested students and educators to access additional information. This book pulls from the research, theory, and practice of individuals who are leading efforts around UDL concepts and AT and instructional technology (IT) strategies. These groups include the Center for Applied Special Technologies (CAST), the Center for Universal Design, the National Center for Accessing the General Education Curriculum (NCAC), the Center for Technology in Education (CTE) at Johns Hopkins University, the Council for Exceptional Children (CEC), and the American Institutes for Research (AIR).

This material was designed primarily as an instructional aid for all teachers who instruct and support students with disabilities. It is also useful, however, to current general education teachers who wish to incorporate UDL methods into their classroom practice, as well as those administrators and others who may be generally interested in the concept of universal design for learning. Universal design for learning integrates different instructional and educational theories with assistive and instructional technology strategies in classrooms. With such a broad base, this guide does not attempt to prescribe one set way of teaching or using a particular product or environment. Rather, it attempts to highlight, organize, and add to existing published literature and resources of UDL.

ACKNOWLEDGMENTS

The Council for Exceptional Children (CEC) and Merrill Education are deeply grateful to Dr. John Castellani of Johns Hopkins University for his extensive review and editing of the manuscript.

We would also like to acknowledge the reviewers who helped to improve the book: Susan Hardin, Assistive Technology Consultant, Macomb ISD and Wendy Murawski, California State University, Northbridge.

In addition, CEC and Merrill wish to acknowledge the contributions of authors to the following chapters:

Chapter 1 *Universal Design for Learning in Today's Diverse Schools*
  Christine Mason and Raymond Orkwis: Council for Exceptional Children

Chapter 2 *Federal Legislation Supporting Universal Design for Learning and Assistive Technology*
  Raymond Orkwis and Christine Mason: Council for Exceptional Children

Chapter 3 *Theories Supporting Universal Design for Learning: Teaching to Individual Learners*
  Christine Mason, Raymond Orkwis, and Robin Scott: Council for Exceptional Children

Chapter 4 *Assistive Technology and Universal Design for Learning in Content Areas*
  Kristine Ruedel, Amie Fulcher, Christina Diamond, Mindee O'Cummings, Stephanie Jackson, and Maurice McInerney: American Institutes for Research

Chapter 5 *Collaborative Strategies for Universal Design for Learning Success*
  Raymond Orkwis and Christine Mason: Council for Exceptional Children

CONTENTS

INTRODUCTION

The process of designing a universal learning environment begins the way any program of curriculum reform does, with the attempt by the teacher to make a positive change for her students. This assumes that the teacher has a clear understanding of what the class needs to learn and how the individual students will be able to learn it. The teacher knows the curriculum and how to best provide for the range of student abilities in a classroom. The teacher considers, for instance, what overall and specific learning goals are most appropriate for what students, what methods of instruction will help achieve those goals, and how students will be assessed.

> The intent of universal design is to simplify life for everyone by making products, communications, and the built environment more usable by as many people as possible at little or no extra cost. Universal design benefits people of all ages and abilities.
>
> ◆Center for Universal Design, North Carolina State University*

Rather than assume that the curriculum taught to the students is necessarily what any particular student is able to learn, the teacher who incorporates universal design for learning understands each student has his or her individual path toward learning. According to the Center for Universal Design, the intent of universal design is to simplify life for everyone by making products, communications, and the built environment more usable by as many people as possible at little or no extra cost. Universal design benefits people of all ages and abilities. The teacher makes use of all available resources, in the classroom and in the larger educational community, i.e., other teachers, school administrators, and parents. To the extent possible, the teacher creates varied and inclusive learning situations that use digital and assistive technologies. She has removed physical barriers to learning so that students with sensory-motor disabilities have more access. She knows how to use such proven teaching methods as differentiated instruction, reciprocal teaching, and peer tutoring. In short, she provides the students access to the general curriculum and supports their progress toward the same standards of learning as their non-disabled peers. The teacher strives to honor the spirit and intent of the Individuals with Disabilities Education Act (IDEA) and *No Child Left Behind* (NCLB).

Universal design for learning is not simply a matter of giving students access to the curriculum, however, and is not primarily the province of special education. As a result of inclusion efforts across the country and the increasing numbers of students with disabilities receiving instruction in the general education classroom, the general education teacher often becomes the facilitator for integrating UDL concepts and special education or assistive technology strategies. The ultimate goal of UDL is to appropriately challenge and effectively engage the full range of students: those with disabilities and those without, those who are average, as well as those who are below and above average. This does not imply that UDL is a "one-size-fits-all" or a "do-it-yourself" solution to learning problems; it is not a panacea but is an achievable process that promotes success for all students working in the general education curriculum and classroom.

As you read about the instructional methods inherent in universal design for learning, you may recognize methods already in place in your classroom. And as you study the origins of universal design for learning in the barrier-free movement, through its incorporation of curriculum-based educational reforms and assistive technologies, to its use of digital instructional materials, it is important to understand that the process of creating the universally designed classroom is gradual and individual. Just as the learning process is unique to each student, the teaching process is unique to each classroom, implying the need to customize our approaches for the best possible fit.

As you read the text, conduct your own self-assessments, as well as school-wide assessments as appropriate.

- *How does this apply to my situation?*
- *Would this improve learning?*
- *How can I integrate technology into a UDL environment?*
- *What would I need to do to implement this?*

By repeatedly asking and answering these questions, you will build a deeper, richer, and more practical understanding of universal design for learning.

Notes

* *http://www.design.ncsu.edu/cud/univ_design/ud.htm.* (Note: For those who want further information on the quotations and text in sidebars and figures, outside sources will be footnoted with the most current URL from the original source. Because of the changing nature of web pages, that URL may be invalid; in that case, an Internet search might be needed.)

1

UNIVERSAL DESIGN FOR LEARNING IN TODAY'S DIVERSE SCHOOLS

In this chapter, you will learn:

- the basic concepts of universal design for learning

- how universal design promotes effective teaching

- the essential features of universal design for learning

- the range of concerns with curriculum and the need for access

- how the general curriculum, universal design for learning, and assistive technology relate to effective teaching

- the differences between instructional and assistive technology and the role that each plays in the universal design for learning classroom

Briarwood: Setting the Stage

Briarwood is a large suburban school district with a diverse student population located just east of the state's largest city. The results of district-wide testing from the previous year indicated lower-than-average student achievement in academic areas across elementary, middle, and high schools across the district. During the summer months, the principal and staff identified strategies to implement in the coming school year for improving school-wide performance. They were introduced to universal design for learning in a two-day UDL training workshop. They also discussed integration of AT devices to accommodate the specific needs of individual students.

As teachers plan for their first few weeks of school, they assess how to integrate into the curriculum concepts of universal design for learning and technology supports. Teachers working with students who have individualized education plans (IEP's) read through these plans to incorporate the use of assistive technology. The teachers work with each other to locate resources to make this task easier and more effective. Spe-

cial and general education teachers collaborate with related services personnel to promote these strategies across classrooms and to integrate the strategies into the special services some students receive. While these teachers and specialists understand how to integrate these strategies, they struggle to make sure that the diverse learning needs of all students are considered while they plan for instruction.

What would you recommend to the educators and specialists to accommodate the diverse needs of students in their classroom?

UNIVERSAL DESIGN FOR LEARNING: THE FOUNDATIONS

The changing face of society is reflected in our schools today. Teachers are charged with delivering instruction to a diverse group of learners who come to the learning experience with a variety of cultures, languages, learning styles, abilities, and disabilities. In today's educational environments, it is common to find not only 100 or more languages spoken in a school, but the integration of diverse learners and students with disabilities in the classroom. Traditional models for instruction need to be expanded to incorporate individual learning styles, prior knowledge about the world in which we live, and accommodations for students who need them. Such classroom diversity heightens the need for inclusive practices. Because the need to demonstrate successful student outcomes has grown more imperative, every teacher can benefit from developing a working relationship with instructional methods and resources to reach the range of students. This is especially important for students with disabilities, who need access to instructional materials and who must be given educational opportunities that allow them to fairly demonstrate what they have learned. For these students to take full advantage of updated teaching practices, curricula, and technological advances, they must have the opportunity to access, participate, and progress in the general education curriculum. *In essence, these students need an environment with the components of universal design for learning, an environment where instruction is flexible, equitable, and accessible every day of the school year.* The vision is that, in these environments, needed accommodations are built into the design of instructional materials. These accommodations will encompass the widespread use of digital curriculum and assistive technologies that have emerged from research and fit the definition of AT in the 1997 Amendments of IDEA, i.e., any item, piece of equipment, or product system that is used to increase, maintain, or improve functional capabilities of individuals with disabilities.

However, just as important to the vision are teachers who are well versed in the methodologies that can result in universal design for learning. These teachers know about, plan for, and incorporate universal design for learning on a routine basis in order to ensure all students access to the general education curriculum.

The greatest promise held by universally designed instruction, that of *flexible, equitable, and accessible ways to teach*, is the wide array of alternatives it provides for teachers. With UDL, teachers can reach each individual student, disabled or non-disabled, providing a platform for each to interact with the curriculum—in ways that best support unique learning styles. With UDL, teachers can implement alternative instruction, speed up or slow down the pace of instruction, or provide the student with alternative ways to demonstrate his or her learning. For example, if a student . . .

- learns best through listening, he or she can use a computer to read stories and information aloud, or to pronounce new words;

- needs hints about where an answer is found, the text (or the computer) can provide prompts about where to look in order to be successful;

- struggles to pick out the most important points, or organize information, he or she can use graphic organizers—on paper or with a computer program;

- learns more easily with large print or without distracting pictures, software can be switched to adjust the size of the text or eliminate graphics;

- can explain things best by using a keyboard and word processor, then that will be the method of choice, rather than pencil and paper; or

- cannot work with a keyboard, he or she will use the device that works best, such as a switch, or voice commands, or other ways that help students share what they know.

Many of the supports provided by universal design for learning are within the realm of special education—and the application of effective technologies, including assistive technology—but ultimately they need to be *inclusive supports for the full range* of students, those who have disabilities as well as those who do not. Given the high percentage of students with special needs who are educated in general education classrooms, the promise of universally designed instruction must be based on instruction that can be delivered by both general and special educators. That is, both general and special educators must be knowledgeable about and proficient in methodologies that support universal access to instruction. More about these methodologies is discussed in Chapter 4. When this understanding is achieved, teachers can collaborate more effectively because all are able to focus on the *implementation* of recommended practices using familiar instructional strategies and readily available modifications.

EFFECTIVE TEACHING IS THE BEGINNING

All students need to have access to the curriculum. However, as we can see in the excerpt to the right, there is a very important distinction between access to information and access to learning. A teacher may present information to students in ways that do not allow students to take in or learn the lesson that lies within that information. A student who has access to information may have the tools to learn but a student who has access to learning knows how to use those tools. Such a student is on the path to self-sufficiency. The excerpt also reminds us that in a universally designed classroom the teacher has not given up control nor has the information she provides diminished in importance. The teacher broadens the delivery of the curriculum with methods that encourage different

> Universal design provides **equal access to learning, not simply equal access to information.** Universal design allows the student to control the method of accessing information while the teacher monitors the learning process and initiates any beneficial methods.
>
> Although this design enables the student to be self-sufficient, the teacher is responsible for imparting knowledge and facilitating the learning process. It should be noted that universal design does not remove academic challenges; it removes barriers to access. Simply stated, universal design promotes **effective teaching.**
>
> ◆Ohio State University Partnership Grants to Improve the Quality of Higher Education for Students with Disabilities
> (*http://www.acs.ohio-state.edu/grants/dpg/fastfact/undesign.html*)

learning approaches by students; in this sense, the teacher facilitates the learning process, which is centered not on a single teaching method but on the students' attempts to gain understanding. The goal of all effective teaching is to promote real learning; understanding the unique contributions of UDL to effective instructional methods is important.

- UDL *assumes a continuum of learning differences* in the classroom; that is, students will learn at levels at, below, and above grade level, and each student has individual areas of strength and weakness;

- UDL relies on the general curriculum that is *presented flexibly, so it includes, engages, and challenges all students appropriately;*

- UDL enables *all students to progress* under the same standards, rather than establishing alternative curricula or standards. It maintains high expectations for all and does not "dumb down" the curriculum for students with disabilities;

- UDL is *inclusive by design:* teaching methods and assistive technologies will be built in or be readily available; they will not have to be added on as afterthoughts by the teacher.

ESSENTIAL FEATURES OF UNIVERSAL DESIGN FOR LEARNING

Two features that are essential to UDL are (1) *the built-in tools that promote access* for the range of learners and, concurrent with the package of accessible materials, (2) *a flexible presentation of the general curriculum* that can meet the needs of individual students. Rose (2002) defines UDL as a curriculum that:

- represents information in multiple formats and media.
- provides multiple pathways for students' actions and expressions.
- provides multiple ways to engage students' interests and motivation.

In this manner, universal design for learning provides a framework for teachers to ensure that instructional strategies, curricula, and assessment are appropriate for a variety of learners to derive benefit from the learning experience. UDL practices promote curriculum flexibility, varied instructional methods, and appropriate assessments that consider learners' diverse needs and prepare them to advance under the general curriculum.

URGENCY FOR PARTICIPATION AND SUCCESS IN THE GENERAL CURRICULUM

A heightened sense of urgency surrounding access to the general curriculum and student achievement has evolved in part from the passage of the *No Child Left Behind Act* (2001). This act requires that the educational plan of each state have challenging academic standards that apply to all schools and all children in the state, including standards for math, reading or language arts, and, beginning in the 2005-2006 school year, science. States are required to show adequate yearly progress toward enabling public elementary and secondary school students to meet the state's achievement standards, while working toward the goal of narrowing achievement gaps. Yearly progress must include a system for measuring the achievement of students with disabilities (NCLB, *Section 1111 (b)*).

The Office of Special Education Programs (OSEP) at the US Department of Education recently conducted a national study with consumer panels to examine issues related to curriculum access (OSEP, 2002). "Greater participation and success in the general curriculum" was selected as the top priority to improve the lives of children with disabilities. Findings from that report indicated, "[g]eneral education and special education stakeholders do not have a shared understanding of the IDEA provisions related to access, participation, and progress in the general curriculum" (p. 26). Moreover, the panel concluded that this lack of clear consensus "undermines policy, research, and practice activities. (page 26)" One key question is, "What constitutes the general curriculum?" Does it include only the district or state-mandated academic study or literacy skills; or could it include additional areas such as communication, orientation and mobility, social, life, and self-determination skills? While these issues continue to be discussed, various states and school districts have interpreted these provisions differently; and many schools have been so focused on the traditional academic curriculum that significant examination of the issues has not yet occurred.

Some of the most critical concerns of general educators, particularly regarding students who fail to achieve, are expressed in an American Federation of Teachers (AFT) publication, *Making Standards Matter 2001*, which urges the creation of an "effective standards-based education system." According to AFT, such a system must include "curricula aligned to the standards, professional development for teachers, help for children struggling to meet the standards, and policies that make meeting the standards count" (p. 5).

Currently all 50 states have statewide academic standards for what students should know and be able to do in academic subject areas. Twenty-nine states and the District of Columbia now have clear and specific standards in the core subject areas of English, mathematics, social studies, and science at three educational levels—elementary, middle, and high school—according to the standards review conducted by AFT (2001). However, almost one-third of the states' tests are based on weak standards; 44% of the tests are not aligned to the standards; and less than one-third of the standards are supported by adequate curriculum. New York is one of only nine states that have 50% of the curriculum components fully developed.[1]

In regard to students with disabilities, the Individuals with Disabilities Education Act (IDEA) Amendments of 1997 requires that these students have access to the general education curriculum and be included in general state and district-wide assessment programs with appropriate accommodations. Data on these students must be incorporated in state and district reports (P. L. 105-17, 20 U.S.C. §1400 *et seq.*). States are also required to develop and report on performance goals and indicators for students with disabilities. A student's individualized education program (IEP) must indicate how the student will be assessed if he or she is not participating in a particular state or local assessment. According to a policy brief disseminated by McREL (Bechard, 2000), public accountability for the learning of students with disabilities serves as a major impetus for schools to use the best instructional methods to enhance the learning of these students.

To have an opportunity to *learn from the general curriculum*, students must first have access to this curriculum. For example, if a student who is blind cannot download reading material from the Web to allow for it to be presented in large print format or in Braille, then that student will be at a significant disadvantage in learning from that curriculum. While in the past teachers have scanned materials into electronic formats or have ordered materials from Talking Books, these approaches are time-consuming and cumbersome. With UDL, such material would be readily available and would not require additional accommodations or modifications by the teacher. Furthermore, if a student with a learning disability cannot read the material in the classroom text, then once again *access to that curriculum* will be restricted. In the past, teachers resolved this concern by tape-recording chapters or asking parents, other students, or volunteers to read to the student; or the student relied for the most part on information gleaned from class lectures and discussions. With UDL, the classroom text not only would be available electronically, but several options might also be available to assist the student at the level that is appropriate for the individual. Not only might the student have access to a text reader, but the degree of support could range from using a software component to reading selected words or phrases or offering the same content material at a reduced reading level. In some instances, other features such as graphic organizers could be embedded into text or an automatic summary provided so that students would have additional prompts about the most important material on an as-needed basis while working with the general curriculum.

WHAT IS THE GENERAL CURRICULUM?

What then is the general curriculum? In an article in AFT's *American Educator*, Kauffman, Johnson, Kardos, Lui, and Peske (2002) define a complete curriculum as including the content, skills, or topics for teachers to cover, a recommended timeline, and instructional materials. They point out that state standards describe academic goals students should achieve. Unlike a curriculum, however, the standards do not include details about specific content, sequence of instruction, instructional materials, or pedagogical methods. However, many districts are relying on these standards as curriculum, rather than as the basis for developing a curriculum. Teachers are:

> . . . often overwhelmed by the responsibility and demands of designing curriculum and planning daily lessons. They entered the classroom expecting to find a curriculum with which they would struggle. Instead, they struggled to develop a curriculum. Whatever confidence they may have had when they entered teaching was undermined daily as they realized that they did not really know what they were supposed to teach, that they had no instructional guides, that they lacked ready access to resources that might enhance their own subject knowledge, and that their private knapsack of instructional strategies was virtually empty.[2]

The ramifications of this confusion for teachers and students can be unfortunate, especially for students with special needs. As Schmidt, Houange, and Cogan (2002) indicate in a companion article, when a coherent curriculum is not available, teachers spend far more time deciding what to teach than how to teach it. And as teachers make decisions—or are unable to make decisions because of time constraints and problems with knowing what to teach—they are having an impact on how students are able to meet the expectations of the general curriculum.

Perhaps one way to consider how to open the general or common curriculum so that students have the opportunity to work toward standards-based goals is to consider the **four main components of a curriculum** as described by the National Center on Curriculum Access (Hitchcock, Meyer, Rose, & Jackson, 2002):

- goals and milestones for instruction;
- media and materials to be used by students;
- specific instructional methods; and
- means of assessing student progress.

Each of the above components represents an area where UDL has potential to increase curriculum flexibility and access. The teacher who knows her students and their needs is on the first step toward creating a classroom founded on UDL principles. Prioritizing instructional goals that range from what every student needs to learn to what some students will learn (see Instructional Pyramid, Chapter 5) is the next step in the process. Deciding on the format for presenting the lessons—that is, what media (high or low technology) and materials will convey information and help students to engage with their learning and to express what they know—comes prior to teaching. Finally, the teacher must decide how to assess students' progress in ways that acknowledge each student's unique style for expressing what has been learned.

While today access to the general curriculum for students with disabilities is largely afforded through "post-hoc adaptations and assistive technologies that help students to bridge the gap . . . the single most significant barrier in the general curriculum is the fixed medium of presentation" (Hitchcock, et al., 2002, p.12). As Hitchcock, et al., indicate, one problem with printed materials—the most common means of providing curriculum—is that they cannot be modified from their original format; nor can the information be enhanced or made more supportive for diverse learners. Moreover, other multimedia formats such as videotapes, audiotapes, and even some software are "also generally 'fixed' in their presentation, making them accessible and appropriate learning tools for some, but not for all."[3] As CAST has indicated, "The central practical premise of UDL is that a curriculum should include alternatives to make it accessible and appropriate for individuals with different backgrounds, learning styles, abilities, and disabilities in widely varied learning contexts."[4]

THE GENERAL CURRICULUM, UNIVERSAL DESIGN FOR LEARNING, AND ASSISTIVE TECHNOLOGY

Technology is inherent in the universally designed classroom. Assistive technologies that benefit individual learners and instructional technologies that meet the diverse needs of groups in classrooms are important for providing the four components of curriculum outlined by Meyer and Rose. Technology is not only a time saver but can enhance curriculum and instruction with built-in adaptations that are central to customizing instruction that takes advantage of student interests, capabilities, and needs. Technology can play a critical role in making curriculum and learning more accessible to students with special needs and others. Students can benefit from the array of supports, both high-tech and low-tech, that digital media offers.

In addition to technologies that focus on instruction, broad-scale technologies like the digital display of text, the Internet, basic word processing, readily available programs, and special assistive technologies are particularly important for individuals with disabilities to access the computer. Assistive technologies play a critical role in making available appropriate accommodations[5] for individuals with disabilities. These accommodations are often provided as special add-ons to enhance an individual's ability to gain access to materials, navigate physical or virtual realms, or communicate.

Many of the technologies used within the UDL framework can be considered effective teaching for all students but a **requirement for some students** to complete basic and advanced learning tasks. As seen in Figure 1.1, a student may require an assistive technology device that is also considered a universal design strategy. Within IDEA, a device or service is identified as assistive technology when it is a requirement for learning; i.e., there is no other way to complete a task except to use a particular device or service. Not all UDL principles can be considered requirements for learning. They may fall under the category of effective teaching, necessary scaffolds, and/or modified examples in order to make sure all students understand a particular educational concept. As a result, identifying an AT device can be different from the identification of a UDL strategy or tool. For example, a student may require an AT device to access a computer while another may simply benefit from this device or tool but not require it. Some students may need high-tech support, such as computers, personal digital assistants, or video devices; other students may need low-tech support, including low-budget, easy-to-create, hands-on materials. Individualized Education Program teams use this decision-making model to categorize AT and then match the AT to specific student functions, usually tied to IEP goals and objectives. In other cases, students with IEP's may not require a strategy to access the curriculum, but do benefit from different learning activities across the school year. In this case, the strategy would not be considered as AT but rather just effective teaching. In addition, not all UDL strategies include technology as a main vehicle for instructional delivery.

For those students who need an IEP, the 1997 Amendments to IDEA require the IEP team to consider incorporating assistive technology devices and services into the student's IEP. Universal design for learning and assistive technology extend the ability of the teacher to meet student needs—UDL by making the curriculum more flexible and assistive technology through providing physical adaptations, devices, and tools to extend the capabilities of persons with disabilities. Both UDL and AT open access to many worlds for individuals with disabilities, though it may not always be apparent whether a technology is classified as UDL or AT. A general rule of thumb is that if it is a device that is added on, rather than embedded in the original design, it belongs with AT. (A further discussion of the legal requirements included in the 1997 Amendments to IDEA is covered in Chapter 2: *Federal Legislation Supporting Universal Design for Learning and Assistive Technology.*)

Designing a universal learning environment is an important step—but only a first step—for teachers striving to provide a positive classroom setting for all students. Teachers who use digital multimedia, for example, can generally accommodate the special needs of diverse learners, including students with physical, sensory, cognitive and emotional disabilities as well as their non-disabled classmates. Effective teachers, though, should recognize the need for additional assistive technology to accommodate the special needs of individual students in the class.

While UDL strategies are designed to support and facilitate flexible ways of learning and a variety of instructional presentation formats, specifically targeted AT implements those strategies by providing appropriate supports to students with individual learning needs. Effectively implementing AT devices and services that accommodate the learning needs of students with

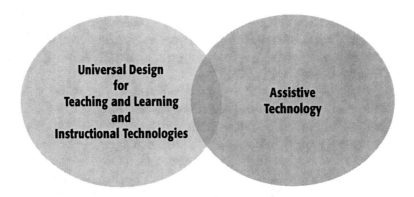

Figure 1.1: The Cross-Over Between UDL and Assistive Technology

disabilities begins with an assessment of student needs based on the context of the classroom and instructional activities. Therefore, the purpose of AT is to provide the necessary accommodations to students so they can participate in the classroom environment to the maximum extent possible.

Figure 1.2 identifies many of the issues effective instructors plan for as they design their lessons—recognizing differences in how students respond to lessons and where accommodations are needed so that the response can be consistent across a continuum of diverse learners.

Teacher Actions throughout the Learning Process	Effective Instructional Methods	Universal Design for Learning	Assistive Technology
Before instruction	• Get to know your students' abilities, special needs, learning styles • After reviewing standards, determine class-wide and individual student learning needs (pretests, review of IEP's) • Devise instructional approaches to reach greatest number of students	• Recognize individual needs of students • Set curricular goals • Determine learning supports • Adapt curriculum and materials to meet individual student needs • Select appropriate UDL strategies, tools, and features to deliver instruction	• Assess student needs • Collect baseline student data • Meet with IEP team to discuss curricular goals and student needs • Make certain AT is documented on the IEP in a manner that is easily understood by any team member • Review IEP recommendations for AT and implement accordingly
During instruction	• Differentiate instruction to reach students on their own levels • Special educator and general educator collaborate • Use other methods [see Chapters 4 and 5] and ongoing feedback loop to adjust instruction	• Use equitable, flexible, accessible methods to fit instruction to student needs • Special educator and general educator collaborate • Use UDL features to determine student progress for feedback and to adjust instruction	• IEP team collaborates to develop action plan for implementation • Student instructed on how to use AT in lessons • Implement AT where necessary • Integrate use of AT throughout UDL instructional strategies
After instruction	• Employ ongoing (or alternate) assessments to determine progress, needs, and future direction of class • Repeat planning cycle	• Make sure assessments reflect UDL characteristics • Assess continuously through variety of formats to track student progress • Adapt delivery of instruction as needed	• Evaluate AT in meeting curricular goals and student needs • Provide follow-up training to students as needed based on lessons learned through implementation • Adapt AT as needed after re-evaluation

Figure 1.2: Implementing UDL and Assistive Technology

Since UDL and AT vary according to the concepts and skills being taught, teachers cannot simply apply one strategy for all students. Rather, individual student needs dictate how curriculum accommodations and modifications must be designed and implemented in the classroom. Teachers must consider, also, that some students may need these strategies every time they complete a task. Other students may use the strategy only until it becomes integrated into the approaches they use to assimilate simple and complex concepts. For example, good readers apply certain processing strategies automatically as they read. Students who encounter difficulties while reading may need support until they learn the strategy and the actual AT tool or device becomes unnecessary. Other students may need this tool or support forever. For the first student, the UDL principles become integrated. In the second example, the AT tool or device remains a part of the student's IEP and classroom accommodation because it is a requirement for functioning.

The principles of UDL provide an excellent environment to support effective implementation of AT. The collaborative nature of UDL, its flexibility, and the embedded supports ease the integration of AT designed to support individualized student needs. Collaborative instructional planning between the general and special educator ensures appropriate integration of AT in all classroom activities and lessons, thereby facilitating access to the curriculum, materials, and instruction by students using AT. Thus, AT is not designed to be something else to learn about in your classroom. Rather, effective implementation of AT involves integration of the device throughout instructional planning and delivery, allowing students to use the tools during classroom activities.

Summary

- UDL provides students multiple means of engaging with the lessons and multiple ways of expressing what they have learned.

- UDL is often enhanced through meaningful integration of assistive and instructional technologies into classroom practice. These technologies are efficient tools for curriculum delivery and individualization and for making modifications that promote independence on instructional tasks.

- UDL requires that teachers become aware of how best to integrate new instructional methods and instructional and assistive technologies into their regular practice and into the day-to-day functioning of their school and community.

- UDL works best when readily available curriculum and technology incorporate its concepts from inception. However, teachers can follow guidelines to intentionally incorporate as many UDL features as are realistic into the materials currently in their classroom and into the ways that they present the curriculum.

QUESTIONS FOR DISCUSSION

1. What content standards or curriculum exist in your state or district?

2. In the Briarwood example, teachers must collaborate while addressing the curriculum, individualized education requirements, and available professional, personnel, and technology resources available in the school. What would be some key features of this discussion?

3. What does curriculum access mean for different groups of students?

4. What can schools and districts do to facilitate the general-special education collaboration needed for curriculum access for *all* students?

Try This!

1. Consider how assistive technology such as ones explained or researched could be a "universally designed feature for learning." Demonstrate how one set of materials provides access and which of its features, if any, are universally designed. Compare and contrast this with how AT would be used to provide access.

2. Research and review a set of state standards in a specific grade-level content area (many standards are available online) and how those standards might consider the needs of students with English as a second language as well as students with and without various disabilities and explain how the components they are reviewing may be useful or may be impediments for these students.

   Then discuss how a school could improve access by adding universally designed instruction for one grade level/topic area.

   Prepare a presentation and discuss the findings. Depending upon the course and content, try to vary topics, grade levels, and subject matter that are covered, so that many different types of materials are reviewed.

   a. Identify features of the materials that appear to be consistent and features that are inconsistent with UDL. Describe how these materials might be changed to be universally designed—what would the textbook publisher need to do to provide universal access?

   b. Review one subject at one grade level, and discuss how the school could deliver universally designed instruction in this area to improve access and promote progress in the curriculum.

Notes

[1] The other states with 50% or more of the components of a fully developed curriculum in place are Alabama, California, Illinois, Kentucky, Massachusetts, New Jersey, North Carolina, and Virginia. Of the other 41 states, 27 have 25% or less of a fully developed curriculum in place. (From the executive summary of AFT's *Making Standards Matter:* http://www.aft.org/edissues/standards/msm2001/downloads/execsummary.pdf)

[2] "Lost at Sea," Kauffman, et al.

[3] (http://www.cast.org/ncac/index.cfm?i=2120)

[4] (http://www.cast.org/udl/index.cfm?i=7)

[5] IDEA '97 defines an *assistive technology device* as "any item, piece of equipment, or product system, whether acquired commercially off the shelf, modified, or customized, that is used to increase, maintain, or improve functional capabilities of a child with a disability" (Part A, Sec. 602 (1).

2

FEDERAL LEGISLATION SUPPORTING UNIVERSAL DESIGN FOR LEARNING AND ASSISTIVE TECHNOLOGY

In this chapter, you will learn:

- the basic legal foundations for Universal Design for Teaching and Learning

- how the civil rights movement assisted with the development of universal design for learning

- the requirements in the 1997 Amendments to IDEA for considering assistive technology

- how legislation contributes to eliminating barriers to curriculum access

Briarwood: Software Necessity or Benefit?

Jorge is a middle school student who is struggling with meeting the basic requirements of reading and math. Ms. Anderson is his eighth-grade teacher. While Jorge is a student with a learning disability, he is integrated into the general education classroom 100% of the day. As a member of Jorge's IEP team, Ms. Anderson understood that tools for Jorge had been designed to facilitate writing skills and to reinforce math concepts. Specific graphic organizer and word prediction software programs were selected as the most appropriate technology for Jorge to use. While working with students one day during a reading comprehension exercise, Ms. Anderson was circulating among the students to check for understanding. She realized that Jorge was effectively using his new technology tools and was able to participate actively with his general education peers. Ms. Anderson also realized that other students in his group were benefiting from the graphically displayed organization of concepts; but for Jorge, it seemed to be a requirement for learning. While Ms. Anderson did not understand the legal issues surrounding how the particular tools were chosen, she knew that for some students, like Jorge, these tools served as a vehicle to promote his functional capabilities, while other students simply benefited from access to different teaching and learning strategies.

How can you differentiate tools that are required to learn versus tools that merely benefit a student in learning?

Inclusive practices, like those in Jorge's classroom, are widely accepted, implemented, and measured; however, teachers, researchers, and school administrators today continue to search for ways to strengthen student achievement while addressing the needs of a burgeoning population of students who are culturally and linguistically diverse, as well as students with disabilities who continue to be included in general education classrooms for up to 100% of their instruction. Under IDEA, students with disabilities are expected to be educated whenever possible in the general education classroom using the general education curriculum. This curriculum access is a major legislative provision in the 1997 Amendments to IDEA. It has had far-reaching implications for both instruction and accountability. General education teachers are now obligated to be part of a student's individualized education program (IEP) team when it is likely that the student's program will be implemented within a general education classroom; students with disabilities must be taught in ways that effectively address their unique needs and that support their progress in the general curriculum; and those students must be included in state and district-wide assessments to ensure that they are progressing in the general curriculum. The No Child Left Behind Act of 2001 (NCLB) raises the stakes even higher for schools. If children with disabilities in a school do not make adequate yearly progress toward 100% efficiency in reading and math over a ten-year period, the school will be held accountable, facing a variety of remedial actions, up to reconstitution and management by a private firm. While NCLB has promoted current efforts to make sure ALL students achieve, a history exists of legislative actions and efforts on behalf of students with disabilities accessing the general education curriculum.

A HISTORY OF LEGISLATION LEADING UP TO NCLB AND IDEA '97

"The time has come when we can no longer tolerate the invisibility of the handicapped in America. . . . These people have the right to live, to work to the best of their ability—to know the dignity to which every human being is entitled. But too often we keep children whom we regard as 'different' or a 'disturbing influence' out of our schools and community activities altogether. . . . Where is the cost-effectiveness in consigning them to . . . 'terminal' care in an institution?"

This statement by Senator Hubert H. Humphrey, made in 1972 when he introduced a bill to include disability in the Civil Rights Act of 1964, underscores the real importance of inclusive practices. The basic civil right to live with dignity and enjoy the freedoms of our democratic society is at the base of this country's Constitution.

Legislation passed during the past several decades has greatly assisted in integrating individuals into the mainstream of economic, social, cultural, and educational life in the United States, people who had previously been segregated because of their cognitive, physical, emotional, and sensory differences. The bill introduced by Senator Humphrey noted above eventually became Section 504 of the Rehabilitation Act of 1973, which first addressed the issue of an appropriate education in the least restrictive environment, meaning that the education for students with disabilities would be comparable to that provided for students without disabilities. This key piece of legislation led to the Education for All Handicapped Children Act (1975), which introduced the concept of individualized education programs (IEP's) for eligible children and provided their parents with the right of redress if they felt that the education services were inadequate for their child's need. This law was later reauthorized as the Individuals with Disabilities Education Act (IDEA), further integrating children with disabilities into the regular classroom and more specifically accommodating their special needs.

UNIVERSAL DESIGN FOR LEARNING AND CIVIL RIGHTS

The Civil Rights Movement of the 1950s and '60s focused the nation's attention on inequalities and injustices in the treatment of a whole segment of our population. This movement proved to be a catalyst for social reflection and change in many ways, including the adoption of federal legislation guaranteeing African-Americans equal access to transportation, voting rights, housing, and economic opportunities. Subsequent legislation extended this guarantee of basic civil rights to individuals with disabilities by prohibiting discrimination and guaranteeing access to appropriate education, among other protections. Throughout the last several decades, there have been renewed efforts to improve the educational outcomes of students with disabilities. IDEA mandates that one way public schools can accomplish this is through involvement and progress in the general curriculum for students with disabilities.

Building on the legislated need to ensure access to public buildings and transportation and communication systems for persons with disabilities, a movement began to grow in the 1970s that attempted to reduce the barriers to and expedite opportunities for physical access. The Trace Center at the University of Wisconsin pioneered research using technology to address communication needs for people with disabilities. A federal program, the National Institute on Disability and Rehabilitation Research (NIDRR), was established in 1978 to fund programs and related activities to "allow… individuals [with disabilities] to perform their regular activities in the community and to bolster society's ability to provide full opportunities and appropriate supports for its disabled citizens."

The Americans with Disabilities Act (ADA) passed in 1990 has been most influential in defining standards for accessibility. As a greater number of expectations have been formed about accommodating the needs of individuals with disabilities, awareness has inextricably linked the civil rights and disability rights movements that began in the 1950s and 1960s to expectations regarding access to learning and instruction.

THE 1997 AMENDMENTS TO IDEA, ASSISTIVE TECHNOLOGY, AND UNIVERSAL DESIGN FOR LEARNING

While IDEA provided access to schools and classrooms and promoted social inclusion in theory, it was only the reauthorization of the 1997 Amendments of IDEA that required students with disabilities to be instructed in the same skills and tasks that were planned for the general school population, and for the first time required IEP teams to consider the need for assistive technology in every student's IEP. While this law did not specify the process for consideration, states and localities have developed strategies for considering AT and matching these devices and services with specific IEP goals and objectives. Frameworks such as the SETT: Student, Environment, Task, and Tools (available at *http://www.joyzabala.com*) and leadership around considerations for use of technology have been developed to guide teams in this process (*see http://www.wati.org, http://www.tamcec.org*, and *http://cte.jhu.edu*).

With the 1997 Amendments to IDEA, there was a discrete and specific mandate to schools to improve results for students with disabilities *through their involvement and progress in the general curriculum.* In defining not only the rights of children with disabilities, but societal obligations to them, the expectation that they will have *access to an education without barriers* has linked this major and historical civil rights legislation to the concept of UDL, or the notion that curriculum can be designed to be barrier-free (Figure 2.1 below illustrates the movement from provision of access to UDL instruction). In turn, the rights of children with disabilities and our responsibility to protect and safeguard their freedoms have linked both UDL and the 1997 Amendments to IDEA in a broader sense to a society without barriers. Current reauthorization efforts include additional considerations of AT devices and services, as well as how UDL should be used in planning for classroom environments that include students with disabilities.

Another critical requirement of IDEA and NCLB is that students with disabilities be a part of the accountability system established for all students and that their scores be included on statewide and standardized assessments, commonly known as Adequate Yearly Progress, or AYP. Schools are now required to include all students in the assessment process as well as to provide appropriate accommodations for these students to facilitate their participation. What this has meant is that for the first time teachers and schools are being held accountable regarding the instruction and learning of ALL students, including those with the most severe disabilities. Moreover, a provision in IDEA requires that parents of children with disabilities receive progress reports that are tied to the goals set out in the IEP, the engine of change at the heart of IDEA. In this way parents can be assured of their child's progress and, because they are part of the IEP team, consider if the student's IEP needs to be modified. As a result, access has become inseparable from learning, as Figure 2.1 and Figure 2.2 demonstrate.

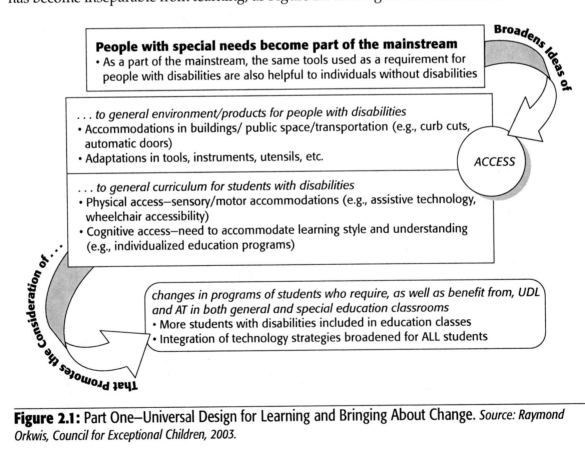

Figure 2.1: Part One—Universal Design for Learning and Bringing About Change. *Source: Raymond Orkwis, Council for Exceptional Children, 2003.*

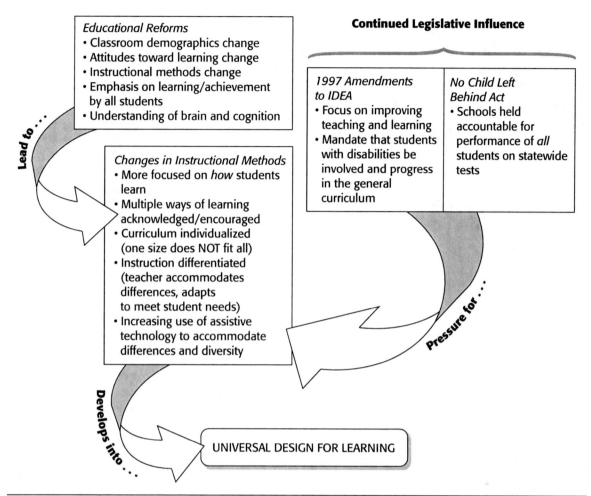

Figure 2.1: Part Two—Universal design for learning in the Changed Educational Environment. *Source: Raymond Orkwis, Council for Exceptional Children, 2003.*

Researchers and disability advocates such as Ron Mace, professor of architecture in the School of Design at North Carolina State University, helped advance disability rights legislation. Dr. Mace founded the NIDRR-funded Center for Universal Design in 1989. He also coined the term "universal design," which has been adapted by the National Center for Accessing the General Education Curriculum (NCAC) as universal design for learning. According to the Center for Universal Design, "the intent of universal design for learning is to simplify life for everyone by making products, communications, and the built environment more usable by as many people as possible at little or no extra cost. Universal design for learning benefits people of all ages and abilities" (2002). This functional definition forms the basis for all explorations of universal design for learning: environments and products are designed from the beginning to provide access to the full range of users, whether or not they have disabilities.

The barrier-free movement seeks to simplify the means for everyone to have access to what they need in their daily lives. It intends to level the playing field for everyone, to allow people with disabilities to be as visible and productive as people who do not have disabilities. The research centers working on these issues have established protocol for physical access and provided technical assistance to guide architects and local and state governments in meeting the legal requirements and expectations for increasing the physical access as well as the performance and productivity of individuals with disabilities.

The Center for Universal Design, National Center on Accessing the General Education Curriculum, and assistive technology groups have played a critical role in setting standards and influencing societal expectations regarding universal design for learning and the removal of physical barriers to access. However, the educational legislation discussed above furthered this agenda by creating the expectation for general education classrooms that curriculum access will result in meaningful learning for *all* students, *including students with disabilities*. Currently, 49 states have adopted state standards, and most districts are assisting schools in bringing standards-based reform to classroom environments. Information about IDEA and current reauthorization can be found at the Council for Exceptional Children (*http://www.ideapractices.org*) and the No Child Left Behind Act can be found at the U.S. Department of Education (*http://www.ed.gov/policy/elsec/leg/esea02/index.html*)

Summary

- Legislation has been the motivator for many of the changes seen in both general and special education. Educators around the country have responded to legal issues by developing policies that support teachers in classrooms and administrators in districts. While policies may differ, they all support the basic civil rights of ALL individuals, including those with disabilities.

- UDL and technology groups have also developed specific strategies for ensuring that there are processes teachers can follow for integrating technology and UDL strategies into the curriculum. While these frameworks are important for providing structure to the legal processes outlined in federal and state legislation, they are not comprehensive.

- Innovative uses of technology continue to change, and the support available to students in classrooms has grown. These comprehensive efforts to ensure access to the general education curriculum for all students have promoted achievement and continue to offer guidance to educators as they design, implement, and evaluate UDL and technology-rich environments.

Questions for Discussion

1. What issues regarding equity and access for individuals with disabilities proved to be catalysts for social and legislative change in the past several decades?

2. The 1997 Amendments to IDEA contain a mandate to improve results for students with disabilities through involvement and progress in the general education curriculum. In what important ways does this mandate relate to the concept of universal design for learning?

3. In the Briarwood example, the teacher recognizes that for some students the software is a requirement for functioning while for others it is just a motivating way to complete an activity. What are some of the ways you would identify students who need it and those who simply benefit from it?

4. What aspects of the basic classroom experience would change with the incorporation of universal design for learning principles into the curriculum?

5. What is meant by "appropriate challenge" when referring to the access provided by a universally designed curriculum?

Try This!

Locate state content standards for curriculum. After identifying these content standards, take one standard and provide one or two examples of how an environment or a product has been designed for universal access in this area, making the standard barrier-free for use by as many individuals as possible. Discuss one or two examples of how a curriculum can be designed for barrier-free access choosing another standard or content area.

3

INSTRUCTIONAL THEORIES SUPPORTING UNIVERSAL DESIGN FOR LEARNING— TEACHING TO INDIVIDUAL LEARNERS

In this chapter, you will learn:

- the principles for Universal Design for Teaching and Learning

- instructional theories that are commonly associated with the design of classroom instruction and fundamental to accommodating students and adapting instruction

- how teachers can use instructional theory to develop instruction

- what is known about UDL strategies and integrating them into individualized learning

Briarwood: Integrating Learning Theory

Ms. Anderson is sharing Jorge's progress with a group of teachers during their shared planning period. She notes other students' interactions with the technology Jorge is using. She talks about how, while planning for each day, she tries to develop different instructional supports to engage students, keep them focused on the main points of the daily lesson, and multiply ways to allow them to show that they have learned the content. In the midst of the conversation, another teacher asks her for a specific framework around her style of teaching or information about different approaches to instruction. Many of the teachers have been teaching for quite some time; and, other than district-related initiatives, they have not had enough time to keep up with the pace of advancing ideas for instruction, specifically for the use of technology. Ms. Anderson shares with the group some frameworks and easy-to-understand charts that help them to understand her ideas about UDL and differentiated instruction. She also reminds them of the technology support available in the building and encourages them to visit her classroom for a few minutes during their

21

planning time to see how the students respond to her teaching style. How would you define your teaching style?

PRINCIPLES OF UNIVERSAL DESIGN FOR LEARNING

In the above example, Ms. Anderson has developed a framework for supporting students in her classroom. This framework is adapted from instructional theory and modified as needed based on curriculum, instruction, and individual student needs. The following framework for UDL has been adapted from the general universal design for learning solutions associated with advances in accessible architecture. Support for this idea was generated during the 1990s with the passage of the Americans with Disabilities Act and has expanded into what we now call Universal Design for Teaching and Learning.

In the 1990s, a working group of architects, product designers, engineers and environmental design researchers collaborated to create a fundamental set of seven principles of universal design for learning as defined by the Center for Universal Design (Figure 3.1) for ease of physical access to products and environments, regardless of the user's ability. The principles are relevant to students with disabilities or special needs in school environments in that they provide guidance in ensuring that all students are able to use curricular materials and to participate in integrated instruction in classrooms that are barrier-free.

In contrast to the universal design of products or environments, universal design for learning expands the focus from the physical world into the broader realm of cognitive and affective access. Some research projects on UDL (cf., the University of Washington's Do-It Project, or the Center on Postsecondary Education and Disability at the University of Connecticut) maintain the format of the principles developed for physical environments to demonstrate the connection between product and curriculum design.

Figure 3.1 clarifies the distinction between the two applications of universal design for learning: the physical principle and the education application.

Instruction can be considered universally designed when, without after-the-fact adaptation, it provides information that is easily recognized by all students, diminishes unnecessary physical effort for access, or is structured to avoid unnecessary frustration and to be highly engaging and motivational for the student. In searching for curricula and materials that are universally designed, the teacher's first job is to consider what barriers will impede a student's understanding and what needs must be accommodated—physically, by assistive technology, for instance, and cognitively, through effective instruction. While universal design for physical environments has ease of access as its ultimate goal, universal design for learning eliminates *only those barriers* that impede an individual's learning. If, in being given access to the curriculum, a student is no longer challenged to apply his or her own strengths to solving problems or demonstrating knowledge—i.e., the learning experience has been made too easy for the student—it is in fact no longer a learning experience. Every student must be challenged; the difficulty is for the challenge to be appropriate to the learner, to engage rather than exclude him or her.

UNDERSTANDING THE RELATIONSHIP OF UDL TO INSTRUCTIONAL THEORY

As teachers begin to practice UDL, they will find that just as the strategies used to organize their instruction help them to prepare for teaching a classroom of diverse learners, their knowledge

Physical Principle	Educational Application
1. *Equitable Use* The design allows all users equal access and avoids segregating or stigmatizing anyone.	1. *Equitable Curriculum* Instruction uses a single curriculum that is accessible to students with widely diverse abilities; curriculum does not unnecessarily segregate students or call undue attention to their "differences." Curriculum is designed to engage all students.
2. *Flexibility in Use* The design accommodates a wide range of individual preferences and abilities.	2. *Flexible Curriculum* The curriculum is designed to be presented flexibly to accommodate a range of individual abilities and preferences; it considers physical and sensory-motor disabilities as well as varied learning preferences and paces.
3. *Simple and Intuitive* The design is easy to understand.	3. *Simple and Intuitive Instruction* Instruction is straightforward, provided in the mode most accessible to students; language, learning levels, and complexity of presentation can be adjusted; student progress is monitored on an ongoing basis to reset goals and instructional methods as needed.
4. *Perceptible Information* The design communicates necessary information effectively to the user, through different modes (pictorial, verbal, tactile), regardless of the user's sensory abilities.	4. *Multiple Means of Presentation* Curriculum provides multiple means of presentation to teach students in ways that will most effectively reach them, regardless of sensory ability, level of understanding or attention; presentation can be altered to meet recognition patterns of individual students.
5. *Tolerance for Error* The design minimizes hazards and the adverse consequences of accidental or unintended actions.	5. *Success-oriented Curriculum* Teacher encourages engagement with curriculum by eliminating unnecessary barriers to engagement; teacher provides supportive learning environment through ongoing assistance, applying principles of effective curriculum design as needed: e.g., teaching Big Ideas, priming background knowledge, scaffolding instruction, etc.
6. *Low Physical Effort* The design can be used efficiently and comfortably and with a minimum of fatigue.	6. *Appropriate Level of Student Effort* The overall classroom environment provides ease of access to curricular materials, promotes comfort, addresses motivation, and encourages student engagement by accommodating varied means of student response; assessment is ongoing, measuring performance; instruction may change based on results of assessment.
7. *Size and Space for Approach and Use* Appropriate size and space is provided for approach, reach, manipulation, and use regardless of user's body size, posture, or mobility.	7. *Appropriate Environment for Learning* Classroom environment and organization of curricular materials allow for variations in physical and cognitive access by students as well as for variations in instructional methods; classroom environment allows for varied student groupings; classroom space *encourages* learning.

Figure 3.1: Educational Applications of the Seven Principles of Universal Design for Learning

and application of effective teaching practices will provide needed options for those students. **Ultimately, it is good practice that will make universal design work:** good design of curricular materials in itself does not ensure effective instruction. As with any tools, materials are only as good as the teachers who apply them. Some of the methods discussed below provide flexibility by offering students alternatives in pacing. Some methods, such as anchored instruction and cooperative learning, for instance, allow students to achieve an independence of learning via alternative groupings in the same classroom; other methods, while not instructional methods per se, offer flexible tools for the teacher, such as models, manipulatives, and technology. No teacher can be expected to use all or even most of these instructional methods; teachers, like students, approach education individually, and not all teachers appreciate or are adept at using certain methods. The secret is for a teacher never to leave students with the feeling that they would have learned more if the lesson had been taught another way.

Differentiated Instruction

The first instructional method to be discussed here is differentiated instruction, a global strategy. Originally used to provide appropriate challenges to gifted students, differentiated instruction can be applied more generally, in response to the differing cognitive needs of students in the classroom (achieving above, at, or below grade level). While the teacher does not change the curriculum itself, she can differentiate the content (concepts to be taught), the process (the method of instruction as well as the means by which students can respond), or the product (how students demonstrate their mastery of the lesson). The teacher makes adjustments in pacing, method of presentation, or degree of complexity of information, which allow students to receive the same content in a manner consistent with their individual abilities and preferred learning modality (Table 3.1) .

In such classes, teachers modify instruction to enhance students' understanding of assignments, and their ability to plan and execute tasks, use materials effectively, comprehend content presented in various media, organize work, understand and use feedback, and express ideas effectively. The goal is to keep individual learners actively engaged and challenged (Tom-

TABLE 3.1

An Example of a Differentiated Math Lesson

To introduce a concept or to initiate the class, the teacher can use whole-class instruction, then use most of the class period for group work, with students working together in small groups of three or four on the concept or skill. Students are assigned to groups based on their current level of readiness for what they are studying, or by their interest in a particular application for the math skill they're studying. They can select from folders that allow them to review homework problems or correct their own quiz from the previous day, packets of file cards with problems at varied levels of difficulty that help them prepare for the upcoming SAT test, a skill review packet with math puzzles directly related to the current unit, a graphing calculator sheet with problems, and a mini-project folder where they create relevant puzzles and problems to be used in the skill review packet. Regardless of what the class is covering, all students are focused on the same concept—but the set of problems each group works on is adjusted to challenge the group.

The teacher can use a tiered assignment with two, three, or four activities at different levels of readiness. There is usually more than one small group working at the same readiness level. Members of each group have their own activity sheet with problems, directions, and additional information as needed. Students work together, helping each other to understand and correct their work. The teacher monitors the students' work, answering questions only if the group members can't figure something out. The teacher changes the membership of the groups almost weekly, drawing on her observations of each student's readiness based on whole-class, small-group, and one-on-one discussions, as well as performance on quizzes.

(Adapted from a lesson at: *http://www.ascd.org/pdi/demo/diffinstr/l1hsex.html*)

linson, 2001). Students can be grouped either by ability or by interests, e.g., kind of intelligence or learning modality.

Cooperative Learning

In a cooperative learning situation, students are clustered into small groups and work in those groups to complete assignments, often staying in the same group for 4–6 weeks. Among the advantages for students with disabilities are increased social interaction, decreased behavioral needs, increased attention to task, and increased physical engagement with task (Eichinger & Downing, 2002; Jones & Carlier, 1995). The use of peer buddies and peer tutors can also facilitate learning in a similar way. With these approaches, peers or members of the cooperative learning group can read to students, help explain concepts, and assist with group projects, as Table 3.2 demonstrates.

TABLE 3.2

An Example of a Lesson in a Cooperative Learning Class

A teacher may utilize the cooperative learning lesson framework to facilitate the completion of a group project or task. A cooperative learning task may follow directed teaching in which the teacher introduces, models, and then provides guided practice with content and skills with the class as a whole.

For example, a teacher may wish to follow up a social studies unit on economics in which topics such as wants and needs, expense, budgeting, cost, income, etc. have been introduced and discussed with the class as a whole. The teacher will have provided opportunities for practice with targeted vocabulary, skills and concepts by incorporating modeling, guided practice, whole class activities, and independent practice in her instructional strategies as she teaches the unit. Next, she may introduce a cooperative learning task to the students in which they will have the opportunity to work together in structured groups to practice and apply knowledge acquired prior to the group work. The teacher would then organize the whole class into groups of four or five students, making sure that the groups are as heterogeneous in nature as possible. The specific cooperative learning task could be to have the students develop a budget using a specified amount of money while considering wants vs. needs, income, expenses, and other concepts defined within the unit. A fictional or non-fictional literature piece may be used to provide an example of finance and budgeting to the whole class prior to each groups' independent work.

Also, the teacher should inform the students of "ground rules" regarding working in cooperative groups to set the climate prior to letting groups work on their own. Discussions regarding interpersonal relations, individual/group responsibility, final product, and evaluation should be clearly articulated in terms of what the students are to do, in what order, with what materials, and what specific learning outcomes the students are to acquire and be able to demonstrate.

When putting together the groups, the teacher may want to consider assigning roles for each member of the group. The teacher may need to explain and model each role so that the students clearly understand how his/her individual task and role will contribute to the success of the whole group. Some roles typically used in cooperative learning groups are:

facilitator—makes certain that everyone contributes and keeps the group on task

recorder—keeps notes on the group's discussions and decisions

reporter—speaks for the group when there is a need to report to the whole class and/or the teacher

manager—distributes, monitors, and manages the group's materials during work sessions

time keeper—keeps track of time to help the group manage their time effectively

As the group work proceeds, the teacher may employ strategies to promote positive social behaviors and attitudes. Interpersonal skills such as conflict resolution, trust building, leadership, constructive criticism, negotiation, consensus, and compromise are important skills to help students develop. Students can be evaluated according to how well they executed their roles and how well they worked with the other group members (individual assessment) and the end product that came about as a result of their work (group assessment).

At the conclusion of the group work, students and teacher should engage in reflective thinking about the group process in terms of if specific learning outcomes were met, group behaviors that promoted successful completion of the task as well as those behaviors which might have hindered the work of the group, and evaluation of the end product.

Thematic Teaching Units

Lessons are centered on a specific theme, but are taught in a number of different content areas that relate to theme, as shown in Table 3.3. Eichinger and Downing (2002) indicate that with thematic teaching, "Language and reading activities related to theme transcend the various content area lessons. . . . lessons taught tend to be very project based. . . . as a result, students are actively engaged in the learning process" (p. 26).

Alternative Instruction/Community-Based Instruction

When it appears that the unit being covered in the class has very little that will be useful or meaningful for a particular student, then the teacher may wish to consider alternative instruction, potentially including instruction in another class or in the community (Agran, Snow, & Swaner, 1999; Schukar, 1997). Community-based instruction may also be an appropriate way to extend a lesson or an alternative way to approach the content being taught in the general education class for specific topics or units (See Table 3.4). This instruction may include service learning, recreation, work experience, or team research (Gent & Gurecka, 1998; Kluth, 2000).

Learning Strategies/Study Skills Approach

Students benefit from being instructed in how to approach their own learning. Receiving instruction on how to take notes, study for tests, and organize their homework, for example, provides students with skills they can use across learning situations. In the most effective

---

TABLE 3.3

An Example of a Lesson Using Thematic Teaching Units

Thematic teaching is grounded in the notion that students learn best when they are able to make real-world connections to a topic. The topic is an identifying theme that unites various content areas, allowing students to learn in a holistic way rather than piecemeal. The teacher (or a group of teachers) decides upon a theme around which all instruction is based.

For example, during the winter season, *snowflakes* may be the thematic unit topic. The teacher would preplan lessons that include readings from different authors about snowflakes. Continuing with the language arts content area, students may write short stories about snowflakes after directed teaching lessons on the writing process or compose original poems after learning about various poem structures and styles. In the science content area, students may study how snowflakes form, capture and examine snowflakes, predict and measure snowfall, etc. Mathematics activities may include lessons on symmetry, the geometry of snowflakes, probability of snowfall, and computation activities using math word problems. Social studies and geography lessons may include activities that involve maps showing areas of precipitation, identifying areas with the greatest snowfall and the least snowfall, as well as understanding how people adapt to snow in their behavior and activities. Students may study winter weather safety and storm preparedness in health education and learn winter sports for physical education. Arts and craft activities may include folding and cutting snowflakes using paper, illustrating students' short stories and poems, and snow photography. Technology may be used to organize and graph snowfall data and design virtual snowflakes. In the music content area, students may listen to songs about snow/snowflakes and incorporate movement or other motor activities.

The integration of the content areas around one theme allows students to see that the things they are learning are connected. Students actively participate in all learning activities by making connections to real-world experiences, working together, and gaining knowledge and skills within a broad framework. Teachers have the flexibility to create and plan interesting activities that allow for a variety of learning styles and provide students with various opportunities to demonstrate what they have learned.

TABLE 3.4

An Example of a Community-Based Lesson

Community-based instruction uses real life situations and settings to enrich the classroom experience. Teachers seek to expand students' understanding and application of skills and concepts learned in the classroom by providing authentic, practical experiences in the community. For example, students who have studied food preparation and nutrition as a unit in health education may as a community-based learning experience have the opportunity to plan and prepare meals for a day. The students will be engaged in planning the menus for a breakfast, lunch, and dinner meal to which parents and other members of the community may come to eat and enjoy during a school day.

After instruction in skills and concepts having to do with food preparation and nutrition, the students will be actively engaged in planning, shopping, preparation, and presentation of three meals to be served throughout a chosen school day. Using knowledge acquired during instruction, the students will apply what they have learned about the effects of good nutrition on the body, the nutritional value of various foods as well as daily-recommended allowances according to food guides. The students will also apply knowledge of meal planning to plan and prepare meals that are nutritionally sound.

Students will be actively engaged in community-based, authentic experiences that will allow them to develop and expand their understanding of learning outcomes identified by the teacher. They may visit a community restaurant to become familiar with menus, food preparation, and presentation. Students will also visit a grocery store to shop for needed food items once menus have been decided. These learning experiences during which students will have actual hands-on experiences will assist the students in developing a deeper understanding of concepts learned in the classroom. During these real life experiences, the teacher's role is to facilitate the transfer and application of knowledge acquired in the classroom to the planned activities in the community helping students to make connections that they may have not otherwise been able to without the use of practical experiences.

examples, students are taught these strategies and then prompted by teachers to apply them. Over a period of weeks the prompts or scaffolds are gradually reduced. For example, if students have been taught about note-taking, the teacher would then conduct several lessons where explicit strategies are used—such as repeating key concepts, using visual materials to reinforce these concepts, as Table 3.5 shows, or even explicitly stating that "this is an important concept that may be on the test."

TABLE 3.5

An Example of a Lesson Using the Learning Strategies/Study Skills Approach

Competent learners have a variety of learning behaviors or strategies available to assist them in acquiring new knowledge. Some learners may need to be explicitly taught strategies that will help them become more successful during the learning process.

A teacher may identify a student who has poor decoding and reading comprehension skills. She may use a problem-solving approach to determine the instructional needs of this student. Appropriate tasks to identify needs may include pre-testing the student, interviewing the student, or examining schoolwork. Once needs have been identified, the teacher may share this information with the student to set learning outcome goals. For a reader struggling with decoding and comprehension, the teacher will identify, discuss, and model appropriate learning strategies before, during, and after instruction with the goal of motivating the student to rely on learned strategies to improve learning outcomes

For example, a teacher presenting a student with newly assigned reading text in language arts class may model strategies for that student to aid reading comprehension. Two common strategies used in reading are *predicting* and *inferring*. The student should be made aware that a good reader will start by making predictions about the text by perhaps reading the title, looking at the pictures, skimming the text, and making connections to personal experiences. The teacher may also model the process of making inferences about text by examining pictures or selected portions of the text. Next, once the student begins to read, he or she may need to develop strategies for decoding new vocabulary. A teacher may introduce and model the *think-aloud* strategy to read an unfamiliar word. This strategy involves asking a variety of questions or using clues to determine the unknown word—*What are other words around this word that can help me predict what it might be? Can the picture(s) help me? What letter does the word start with/end with and how do I make that sound? Can I sound the word out? Do I know other words that look like this word?*

(continued)

TABLE 3.5 *Continued*

A student may also be made aware of other techniques that good readers use before, during, and after reading. The teacher may model *fix-up strategies* for a student to help him or her become aware of other ways to aid comprehension such as rereading the text, rereading surrounding text, skipping over the text to come back later, making a reasonable guess until further information is obtained, etc. At the end of reading, the teacher may model techniques such as finding the main point or main idea, determining the author's intentions or purpose, reflecting on the text, and summarizing the main points.

Study skills and strategies may also be explicitly taught to struggling students. Techniques such as memory strategies, mental imagery, note-taking, graphic organizers, SQ3R, time management, and goal setting, to name a few.

Other related instructional strategies and examples from the National Center for Accessing the General Education Curriculum are listed below and included in Tables 3.6 and 3.7.

- Concept maps are visual and graphic representations of information that show both small units of information and the relationship between these units. Concept maps—also known as story maps, graphic organizers, advance organizers, story webs, semantic maps, and cognitive organizers—are often used to teach text structure, to aid comprehension, and to help students understand vocabulary.

- Anchored instruction is an approach for instruction and exploration that occurs in a shared environment. All activities in an anchored learning environment are designed around a realistic situation or "anchor" in which there is a problem to be solved by the group. For example, students could study the effects of different weather conditions on plants by growing plants under a variety of conditions, charting and tracking the weather, simulating the weather conditions, and observing how the plants respond.

- Modified text is any text that has been changed from its original form. For this review, modified text refers to text content, not physical characteristics such as size, font, or color. Text content can be modified by rewriting the text for readability—such as shortening sentences or substituting simpler words for more difficult words. Another technique for modifying text content is to provide support in the form of hyperlinks that explain difficult vocabulary or text structures.

- Text to speech is any process or product in which a student is exposed to printed text while hearing it read aloud. For this study, text-to-speech refers to the reading of text from a computer screen using synthesized (computer-generated) speech or digital (human-recorded) speech.

- Manipulatives are objects that are used to convey abstract ideas or concepts. Manipulatives include an array of items such as tangrams, number cubes, 3-D models, topographical globes, puzzle maps, story-character puppets, and word or letter cards.

- Simulations and virtual reality both allow students to experience a real life situation in an artificial environment.

- Simulations are activities that can be conducted in person or on a computer. In a person-based simulation, students might set up a class store or lemonade stand as a way of learning about money and the factors that influence supply and

TABLE 3.6

An Example of Lessons Using Other Instructional Strategies: Part 1

Concept Mapping

The acquisition of meaningful learning involves the assimilation of new concepts into a student's existing cognitive structures. Meaningful learning takes place when a student consciously and explicitly ties this new knowledge to relevant concepts that he or she already possesses.

One of several purposes for which concept mapping is used can be to aid and/or assess understanding of information previously taught. A teacher may wish to introduce a concept-mapping task during a unit on *weather*. A component of the lesson may include information about clouds. To evaluate students' level of understanding, the teacher may initiate a guided learning task using concept mapping to review the vocabulary and concepts related to information learned about clouds. A "spider" concept map graphic organizer with nodes and links can be given to students to assist in organizing information. The teacher can guide students through completing the map by modeling and asking relevant questions to allow students to demonstrate their understanding of the information. For example, students may fill in the central oval of the concept map with the focus word *clouds*. Next, the teacher can ask questions related to information previously taught. Questions can relate to the names of the various types of clouds, characteristics of the different types of clouds, weather patterns reflected by different cloud formations, etc. This information can be added to the other nodes on the concept map with links that describe the relationship between the nodes. Once the concept mapping is completed, students could begin a writing task that requires them to utilize the ideas from the graphic organizer to develop a well-formed, multi-paragraph report on *clouds*.

Teachers now have available concept-mapping software to assist them in developing lesson plans to explain new concepts, describe relationships, and have students develop their own concept maps using a variety of graphic organizers.

(Adapted from a lesson at: *http://www.canteach.ca/elementary/inform2.html*)

Anchored Instruction

This instructional strategy involves putting students in the context of a problem-based story. The students "play" an authentic role while investigating the problem, identifying gaps to their knowledge, researching the information needed to solve the problem, and developing solutions. For example, the students may play the role of pioneers on the Oregon Trail. The teacher facilitates and coaches the students through the process of researching, organizing, synthesizing, and analyzing information based on the real-life experiences of the early pioneers. Relevant goals for a lesson based on life on the Oregon Trail could consist of identifying and understanding cultures and customs of the early pioneers; understanding the contributions of various groups in establishing a community; recognizing relevant issues, events, people, and developments in U.S. history; and understanding how the physical environment affects people's lives.

This anchored instruction activity would lend itself well to cooperative learning tasks as a component of the unit. Also, the teacher may find that many of the unit activities can address the variety of learning styles that students possess. Activities may be tailored to allow for the demonstration of learning through multiple intelligences as well.

Technology can play an integral part of anchored instruction for this activity through the use of the Internet and software programs for researching, writing, and creative projects based on the Oregon Trail experience and history.

(Adapted from lesson at: *http://avln.org/resources/projects/carmenmagray.pdf*)

---

demand. Using computer-based simulation software, students might create and manage all aspects of planning and running a city.

- Technology tools are any technological device or program. They include videotapes and video disks, audiotapes, computers, computer software, GPS systems and so forth.

- Models are samples of content, process, or product that serve as exemplars for students. Models can be used as part of instruction to demonstrate an acceptable or exemplary product, such as an essay. They can also be used to shape a desirable performance, such as a "think aloud," in which a teacher models the use of a strategy, or a process, e.g., the stages in the writing process.

TABLE 3.7

An Example of Lessons Using Other Instructional Strategies: Part 2

Simulations and Virtual Reality

Simulations allow the teacher to provide an experiential situation for students that realistically portrays ideas, concepts, and skills necessary to acquire the target educational outcomes.

A teacher may introduce a social studies unit on colonial life by asking students to imagine what life was like for children in colonial schools. After directed teaching lessons on colonial life in general and colonial school life specifically, the teacher can introduce the simulated learning component of the unit as the culminating activity. The target educational outcomes can focus on facilitating the students' understanding of history, comparing and contrasting colonial schooling with present-day schools, and role-playing or simulating the life of a student in colonial times.

After thorough research of colonial school life, the teacher and students will arrange/decorate their classroom to look like a typical classroom in a colonial school. A school day can be designated as "Colonial School Day," with students dressing in the attire of colonial schoolchildren. The students should be able to demonstrate their knowledge and understanding of colonial school life by their actions during the day. Activities could include specific role-play situations based on prior reading of fictional text or student-created plays, simulation of food, games, and materials used during the period, journal writing, and other teacher-planned specific activities that will help students conceptualize and integrate knowledge as well as make real-world connections.

(Adapted from lesson at: *http://www.lessonplanspage.com/SSColonialAmerica-SimulatedColonial School46.htm*)

UNDERSTANDING HOW WE LEARN

As advances are made in science, educational researchers can now actually look at the brain as individuals engage in various learning tasks. Temple, et al. (2003) state: Seeing the effect of interventions on brain function[1] allows researchers to better understand and treat disabilities based on dysfunction. It also provides a basis for understanding that learning patterns are unique and that by stimulating the centers of greatest mental activity in each student a teacher enables that student to follow how the brain processes information.

Research supports the notion that some individuals learn by making connections with what they're feeling or observing, with what they sense about the world, constantly asking *Why.* Other individuals learn by listening to and analyzing information, looking for facts and wanting to know the reasons behind everything. Others process information best when moving about or physically creating something; they want to know how things work by taking them apart and putting them back together. Yet others need to dramatize their learning or discover possibilities hidden in the question, *What if?* These questions reveal learning styles for the particular tasks. These learning styles are not just a matter of personal preferences, they are the natural paths students use to create meanings. As we consider this knowledge about how brains operate, however, it is important that we do not overreact and unfairly or unnecessarily overcategorize students, pigeonholing them as "visual or auditory learners," for example.

Recent findings show that an individual's most efficient learning style may change with the specific task and/or where she is in the learning process. For example, a particular student may learn most effectively by first talking with someone else about an idea. As the individual becomes more knowledgeable, learning efficiency may shift; and the fastest learning may then occur when the person reads about, writes about, or actually tries to implement the idea. The most effective teachers will focus on how students respond to wholes as well as parts, on how they can generalize from knowing how the parts of a concept fit together, e.g., the relationship between phonics and meaning of words, "because the brain naturally links local neural activity to circuits that are related to different experiential domains."[2]

People who are engaged in learning in a mode they are most comfortable with experience more neural and chemical activity in their brain—in short, they are thinking better. In their work, Renata and Geoffrey Caine (1991, 1997) examined the physical and psychological impact of stress and challenge on student response and the effect of the learning environment on what students learned: how, for instance, did students respond during structured activities and active experiences; and how did the outcomes of memorization by students differ from their construction of meaning? In their synthesis, the Caines outlined twelve principles of learning. The basic tenet of those principles is that *learning is most effective when the brain puts memories and experience into a whole*, that is, when information is embedded in rich and meaningful experiences. Meant as an alternative to the more mechanical method of lecturing from a textbook, these principles share with universal design for learning a student-centered orientation: they ask a teacher to fit instructional skills and content to the learner's individual approaches, rather than make the learner fit into an inflexible curriculum.

Their view is also holistic: the classroom environment can either facilitate or impede the learning process.[3] Students react physiologically to a classroom that is bright, well-lit and, most important, a safe place to learn, since stress inhibits the learning process. The physical environment should be as flexible as the curriculum; students should be able to move about and immerse themselves in different activities and different groupings.

Brain Research

Brain research indicates that higher-order brain centers that process complex, abstract information can activate and interact with lower-order centers, as well as vice versa. For example, teaching students simple emotional expressions (vocabulary and idioms) can take place in the context of talking about different emotions and what situations elicit different emotions. Students' vocabulary acquisition can be enhanced when it is embedded in real-world complex contexts that are familiar to them. Finally, students need time and experience ("practice") to consolidate new skills and knowledge to become fluent and articulated.

By implication, brain research confirms what we know from education research: that educators must make provisions for individual differences in learning styles. Instruction for beginning language learners, Individual differences in learning style may not be a simple matter of personal preference, but rather of individual differences in the hardwiring of the brain and beyond individual control.

◆From *Brain Research: Implications for Second Language Learning*, Fred Genesee, McGill University; ERIC Digest EDO-FL-00-12, December 2000; at: *http://www.cal.org/resources/update.html*

HOW THE NATURE OF LEARNING INFLUENCES INSTRUCTION

Research has provided us with tools for understanding how to improve learning efficiency and enable teachers to enhance learning conditions for students who may have very different learning histories and experiential backgrounds. To best customize learning to meet learner needs, teachers will benefit from considering learner engagement, how to make learning an active and interactive experience for students and how to add the flexibility needed to be responsive to individual students. Some of the key concepts derived from existing research and theories regarding learning and their influence on instruction follow. *How could classroom instruction vary if you considered these components of learning in planning daily lessons and longer instructional units?*

Learning Is an Active Process

- Students are active learners, who process, analyze, and examine experiences for the learning value. Students and teachers work together in the pursuit of understanding.

- Experience shapes the brain. We make connections (literally, in the brain) between experiences and what we learn; thus, interaction provides an effective way to learn.

Traditional Learning	Universal Design for Learning
Learning Is a Passive Process • Teachers "own" information and dispense it to students as a "product" • Teachers "stand and deliver" instruction; the information and the instruction is the same for everyone • Students learn through memorization, drill, and testing; they passively absorb information	*Learning Is An Active Process* • Teacher is facilitator of learning, essential to learning but not center of classroom; teachers don't "own" the lessons • Students interact dynamically with information; learning is personal because it begins with individuals • Memorization is integrated with experiences, through which students process, analyze, examine to discover/create meaning
Instruction Demands All Of Students' Attention • Students' personal reactions to lesson are not of prime importance • "Time on task" is important • Instruction geared only to logical functions	*Instruction Is Engaging* • Lessons are structured to involve students' natural thinking processes and interests • Instruction is geared to whole person
Instruction Is Homogenous • Students adapt to curriculum that is delivered in one way, allowing for little flexibility	*Instruction Is Individualized* • Skills and content made to fit learner, not learner made to adapt to curriculum
Educational Environment Is Not A Major Consideration • Order and unity (i.e., a quiet classroom) are sought	*Educational Environment Is Safe* • Personal exploration encouraged, rewarded • Authentic assessments move focus from "success" to real learning

Figure 3.2: COMPARING TRADITIONAL LEARNING TO BRAIN-BASED LEARNING

- Physical activity and other varied experiences can promote the growth of mental functions by stimulating different parts of brain, enhancing connections between neurons.

- Individuals need to be appropriately challenged (see Zone of Proximal Development on following page): too much challenge (or challenges that are perceived as "unsafe") and the brain "down shifts" so the student learns less; too little challenge and the brain "goes elsewhere" to more interesting (i.e., self-determined) places.

- Emotion is an important catalyst in the learning process; thus, the feeling of safety is an enhancement to learning.

People learn best when solving realistic problems in real-world applications. Learning should be part of an experience larger than the passive reception of facts.

Learning Is Engaging

- Learning is a natural and ongoing part of individual function; it happens constantly in everyone as we take in and process information.

- Learning requires engagement. Students want to make sense out of experience; they need to function efficiently in their environments—both of these are basic survival instincts.

- Learning is cumulative and developmental (see the discussion of Vygotsky's Zone of Proximal Development, on following page); students use what they already know to build new knowledge.

- Learning involves both focused attention and peripheral perception, conscious and unconscious processes. The brain not only absorbs information of which the person is aware, it also absorbs peripheral information below the level of conscious awareness.

Learning Is Individualized

- Students need to understand the world from their own unique vantage points; different approaches to learning stimulate "active processing of experience."

- Student preferences should be considered when teachers adapt the instruction for individual students: for some students, rote learning is useful and for some it is "drill and kill."

- Rehearsal and review help students minimize the natural decay process for retaining information.

Learning Occurs in a Safe Environment

- Students are available for learning when they are certain of their physical safety.

- Students take learning risks when they know they are accepted and respected as persons of worth.

- Students learn when they know that their contributions are valued.

- Students progress when they engage in academic inquiry in a non-judgmental culture.

ZONE OF PROXIMAL DEVELOPMENT

Recent knowledge about how the brain functions supports Vygotsky's theory (1978) that social interaction is fundamental to the development of cognition and that voluntary attention, logical memory, and formation of concept evolve through two stages—first between people and then inside the child; full development of a concept depends upon full social interaction. He called the optimal relationship between the material to be learned and learner characteristics the *zone of proximal development* (ZPD) and defined it as "the distance between the actual developmental level as determined by independent problem solving and the level of potential development as determined through problem solving under adult guidance or in collaboration with more capable peers" (1978, p.86). In other words, the ZPD is the difference between what a student can do on his own and what he can do with the guidance of a teacher or a more knowledgeable peer. The ZPD is the general cognitive area in which learning occurs; it is a constantly permeable and, ideally, a constantly progressive boundary. When students are in their zone, learning is at its most efficient. According to the theory of the ZPD:

- Since every student works at his/her own level of development, every student needs a different amount of support to move from that proximal into a new level.

- New information is connected to previously learned information.

- Learning is connected to present knowledge, which is connected to what a student is able to learn. A good teacher can work with a student to move that student into the next step or level, or peers who are working at a level slightly above a student having difficulties can work toward the same end.

Because of the gap between what a student believes he or she can achieve and what the teacher believes to be the upper limits of that student's capabilities, instruction should ideally challenge the student to move that boundary. This implies that the teacher knows the student's individual interests and preferences for interacting with the material/information to be learned, and it assumes that the teacher can retain sufficient flexibility in instruction to engage the student. The teacher's role, then, is to be aware of appropriate challenges: if they are too difficult, the student becomes confused and unable to learn (the "down shifting" noted above); if they are too low, the student is not challenged and does not learn. A teacher who incorporates the ZPD as part of her teaching repertoire would be building an environment based on UDL principles and adhering to the mandate of IDEA for students to be involved and progress in the general curriculum.

MULTIPLE INTELLIGENCES: IMPLICATIONS FOR THE UDL CLASSROOM

Because the path to knowledge is unique to each learner and to specific learning tasks, the teacher must know the best way to clear the path, so to speak, to allow the student to use his or her natural inclinations to form meanings and to support learning. It may also be valuable to examine the research and theories of Howard Gardner in regard to multiple intelligences. The importance of Gardner's work is the richness it suggests for the learning environment. Rather than viewing learning as primarily an academic task dependent upon reading to be followed by paper-and-pencil tasks, Gardner has opened up a world of alternative ways to approach instruction, based on learning characteristics of the individual learner. Basing his findings on the study of cognitive development, Gardner characterized intelligence as "the ability to solve real-life problems, generate new problems to solve and to make products or offer needed services in one's culture" (Gardner, 1982, 2000). Intelligence, he maintains, is multi-faceted, divisible into at least eight distinct types: verbal/linguistic, logical/mathematical, musical, spatial, kinesthetic, intra-personal, interpersonal, and naturalistic intelligence. (See Figure 3.3.)

Each of these intelligences is important and addressing them can foster student engagement. This must be done, however, in a culture where traditional teaching strongly emphasizes verbal/linguistic and logical/mathematical at the expense of the others.

In reviewing Gardner's approach to instruction, it becomes clear that he does not place greater importance on one intelligence over any other; nor does he imply that it is undesirable to teach linguistic and logical skills—a teacher who can encourage these skills in students will be contributing to the future success of those students *because* our culture so values those qualities. By broadening perspectives on the different ways of knowing and thinking, educators can design more effective classroom experiences.

Multiple intelligence theory is not a prescription for teaching all things at all times to any particular student. Gardner warns against using these multiple paths to knowledge to pigeon-hole a student into always responding to the curriculum in the same manner. That is, a student who demonstrates musical intelligence should not be encouraged to only respond through music or movement but should be taught to develop his other intelligences, particularly those that will be tested. Pragmatically, a student cannot dance his way to a good grade on a standardized exam. But if teachers place less emphasis on passive learning and more emphasis on alternate ways of learning, including movement, manipulation of objects, music, and social interactions, they will utilize student strengths. These teachers can show students how to use their more developed intelligences to learn subjects that would normally only employ their weaker intelligences; a naturally engaged student will invest more effort and be more open to understanding.

Teaching to multiple intelligences or, for that matter, using any alternative instructional methods, should not be done indiscriminately. Understanding the individuality of the student is inherent in understanding what UDL methods will best promote learning. Gardner himself has responded to the risk of misapplication of his theory, warning against ill-considered or unnecessary application of multiple intelligences and the use of multiple intelligences as evaluative criteria. Teachers should not attempt to teach all subjects to all intelligences nor have students go through the motions of one or more intelligences. Superficial or inappropriate use of multiple intelligences not only trivializes the benefits but also can be counterproductive to learning.

Type of Intelligence	Educational Applications
1. Verbal/Linguistic Intelligence • Students exhibit strength in reading, writing, speaking, and conversing in one's own or foreign languages • Students with strengths in this intelligence respond to traditional teaching and traditional assessments	• Text-based learning, verbal responses • Reading, memorization, writing, talking, debating • Word games and puzzles
2. Logical/Mathematical Intelligence • Students are strong in number and computing skills, recognizing patterns and relationships, timeliness and order, and the ability to solve different kinds of problems through logic • Students typically do well in traditional classrooms where teaching is logically sequenced and students are asked to conform	• Problem-solving and experimentation; question and answer work • Classification, categorizing, patterning, working with abstract • Organizers: matrices, charts, tables
3. Visual/Spatial Intelligence • Students visually perceive their environment; like to see what teacher is talking about • Students create and manipulate mental images • Student strengths are in reading, studying maps and charts, drawing, using mazes and visual puzzles, imaging things	• Images reinforce concepts and communicate complex notions • Maps and models, graphs, diagrams, visual organizers, multimedia resources • Design, draw, daydream, look at pictures
4. Bodily/Kinesthetic Intelligence • Students have good physical coordination and dexterity; use fine- and gross motor skills, and express themselves or learn through physical activities • These children are sometimes labeled "overly active" in traditional classrooms where they are told to sit still and learn	• Full-body activities; acting and physical contact (touching materials) • Role playing and simulations • Use of tools and crafts
5. Musical Intelligence • Students understand and express themselves through music and rhythmic activities or dance; they compose, play, or conduct music or use rhymes • Student strengths: singing, picking up sounds, remembering melodies, rhythms • It is easy to overlook children with this intelligence in traditional education	• Rhymes, raps, melodies, jump rope songs • Mnemonic devices, performing and listening to music or rhythmic poetry
6. Interpersonal Intelligence • Students easily understand how to communicate with other people and how to work collaboratively • Student strengths are in leading, organizing, resolving conflicts, and communicating • They may have been identified as talkative or " too concerned about being social" in traditional classrooms	• Use teams or cooperative groups; encourage sharing, comparing, relating, interviewing • Minimize lectures, isolated quiet work

Figure 3.3: Educational Applications of Multiple Intelligences

Type of Intelligence	Educational Applications
7. Intrapersonal Intelligence • Students easily understand their inner world of emotions and thoughts • Student strengths: recognizing strengths and weaknesses, setting goals for self • Students may tend to be more reserved but are intuitive about what they learn and how it relates to them	• Provide opportunities to reflect, work alone, pursue interests, incorporate new learning on their own • Self-paced projects, computer-based work
8. Naturalistic Intelligence • Student's strength is understanding the law in the natural world • Students may tend to feel comfortable outdoors • Students easily learn from nature and the natural world	• Provide opportunity to engage in activities outside; encourage nature visits and activities pertaining to the environment

Figure 3.3: (Continued)

THE RELATIONSHIP OF BRAIN RESEARCH TO UDL AND ACTIVITY-CENTERED LEARNING

Our understanding of multiple intelligences and ZPD and our most recent knowledge from the field of brain research support two beliefs that are central to universal design for learning: (a) because every brain has unique patterns of development, all students learn differently; and (b) students learn best when they can engage with their learning, when they feel safe and care about the information. Teachers who recognize individual differences in the classroom and focus their instruction on minimizing student weaknesses and utilizing their strengths—rather than teaching all students in a strict textbook/lecture style—connect to students' natural paths to knowledge and create an atmosphere that allows for education to be a participatory experience. Such teachers then become learning coaches, whose primary task is setting the educational stage for student learning rather than delivering instruction.

One way to realize the educational implications of how the brain functions is to observe students as they are placed in different instructional situations. With this approach, teachers observe how the individual student reacts to instructional tasks in the context of how the human brain *recognizes information* (sometimes known as recognition networks), how it *uses information* (called strategic networks), and how it *reacts to information* (affective networks).[4] With this methodology, teachers consider the best options for providing instructional *input,* options for how the student *interacts* with the material/information to be learned, what the student *enjoys,* and how the student prefers to *demonstrate* what she has learned.

Activity-Centered Learning

An approach that assists teachers in planning assignments so that UDL components facilitate learning in a context of how the brain works is Activity-Centered Learning based on Gifford

The Learning Brain

Learning requires complex interactions of the recognition, strategic, and affective systems. No two brains learn in exactly the same way. While everyone's brain functions take place in roughly the same areas and work together in roughly the same way, Positron Emission Tomography (PET Imaging) studies have shown that each individual has his or her own activity "signature."

Each of us has a different functional allocation of cortex. For example, some people have larger regions devoted to recognizing patterns, generating strategies, or focusing on particular priorities. These differences seem to be reflected in different types of learning styles, strengths and weaknesses, and varying "kinds" of intelligence (see the work of Howard Gardner).

Thinking about individual differences in light of the three brain systems can help us understand the ways in which curriculum must be flexible to reach all learners. Multiple representations of content can adjust to the recognition systems of different learners, multiple options for expression and control can adjust to the strategic and motor systems of different learners and multiple options for engagement can adjust to the affective systems of different learners.

◆(From "The Learning Brain," at: *http://www.cast.org/udl/TheLearningBrain10.cfm*)

and Enyedy's (1999) Activity Centered Design (ACD). Activity-Centered Learning is a combined learner-and-activity-centered approach. With this approach, student characteristics, as well as knowledge regarding desired learning outcomes, are considered in designing flexible learning activities. With the focus on high-stakes assessment, this approach may be particularly valuable for teachers working with diverse student populations to meet state standards of learning.

Consistent with Vygotsky's theory of proximal development, Gifford and Enyedy's (1999) Activity Centered Design (ACD) provides a learning context that is considered a process "in which an individual's cognition is defined by its relation to the material setting and the forms of social participation encouraged in these settings" (p. 1). With ACD, learning is reconceptualized as learning to participate within a cultural context mediated by one's interactions with others; i.e., it is conceptualized as a continuum beginning where one's participation is influenced primarily by more capable others (Vygotsky, 1978) and the physical constraints imposed by the physical world (Hutchins, 1995), ending at higher levels with fuller, more independent participation.

In a recent National Academy of Sciences text on achieving high standards, Ready, Edley, and Snow (2002) portray learning as being best facilitated through an interface among learner-, knowledge-, and assessment-centered instruction. They state, "In knowledge-centered learning environments, the content, organization, and sequencing of curricula are carefully constructed to facilitate students' development of a deep understanding of the subject matter." (p. 34).

When the knowledge-centered environment includes a focus on learning activities, recognition is given to the importance of the journey, i.e., the impact of the activity being used to teach a particular skill or concept.

◆(*http://books.nap.edu/books/0309083036/html/29.html*)

The ACD framework

- Puts the onus on educators to create environments and use materials and pedagogies that *support* the highest level of capability of the individual, providing supports to the degree that is necessary but not creating false dependencies or lowered expectations.

- Considers learning within the context of the community, recognizing the importance of the interplay among learner, knowledge, and assessment.

With this approach, instead of placing the learner or the teacher at the center of the model, researchers design activities to help learners develop the "ability to carry out socially formulated, goal-directed action through the use of mediating materials and social structures" (p. 6). In Activity-Centered Learning, students move from being partial participants, with considerable dependency on others and on mediation tools, to full participants, more able to flexibly engage in interactions in their environments.

Using UDL with an activity-centered approach, students are provided options for learning. They are also provided supports (both human and material), recognizing that much learning occurs in the context of social interactions and that interactions with others are instrumental in facilitating learning. So, if students were learning about rain forests as part of a science ecology unit, they would be provided with activity options for how they wanted to learn initial information about that topic, how they wanted to research that topic, and how they would demonstrate that they have mastered skills and concepts. Teachers then would use UDL tools as well as make decisions about how to involve peers, aides, and themselves in facilitating the learning.

Summary

- Information about how individuals learn is important for a complete understanding of how to integrate current learning theory. This information helps teachers to use research on how brains process information and respond to stimuli.

- Teachers can apply information about zone of proximal development and multiple intelligences theories to structure more effective learning for students and better teaching for educators.

- By understanding brain-based learning theories, educators can be better prepared for teaching students utilizing instructional theories to augment UDL.

Questions for Discussion

1. In the Briarwood example, it is important to recognize that instructional theory needs to be considered when designing curriculum. Based on the theories presented in this chapter, which instructional theories do you think directly impacts what Ms. Anderson is doing in the classroom?

2. What strategies would you use to identify the relationship between learning, how individuals learn, and optimizing the learning situation?

3. What is the role of the zone of proximal development in engaging students?

4. What is the importance of brain research to "learning efficiency"?

5. What does our knowledge of multiple intelligences contribute to our understanding of how to engage students in the learning process?

5. How does a Learner-Activity-Centered approach complement ZPD and recommendations to use UDL?

Try This!

1. Develop a typical lesson and describe a number of approaches that will allow students to react to it according to each of the multiple intelligences. Using the principles of brain-based learning and multiple intelligence, determine how such a lesson can be individualized for different learners, what can be changed to make the lesson experiential for students and what elements of your instruction would make it "safe."

2. Considering the examples of instructional methods described in this chapter, what specific features of each allow for diversity among students in their learning styles and ability to demonstrate what they have learned?

3. According to a survey conducted by the National Center on Accessing the General Curriculum (NCAC), teachers presently use a variety of common enhancements to the curriculum to accommodate for the needs of students. Describe how features of these common enhancements relate to the concept of UDL in terms of:

   - opportunity for individualization of learning materials
   - flexibility in teacher presentation

Notes

[1] A recent study at Stanford University, for instance, analyzed the effect of educational interventions on brain function in children who exhibited dyslexia by studying MRI images before and after the interventions (see: *Neural deficits in children with dyslexia ameliorated by behavioral remediation: Evidence from functional MRI*, Temple, E., Deutsch, G.K., Poldrack, R.A., Miller, S.L., Tallal, P., Merzenich, M.M., Gabrieli, J.D.E. *Proc. Natl. Acad. Sci.* U. S. A. 2003 100: p. 2860-2865).

[2] *Brain Research: Implications for Second Language Learning*, Fred Genesee. ERIC Clearinghouse on Languages and Linguistics, December 2000, ERIC Digest # EDO-FL-00-12; *http://www.cal.org/ericcll/digest/0012brain.html*.

[3] For further information about the effect of the classroom environment on learning and accommodations for special needs, see the work done by Adaptive Environments (*http://www.adaptiveenvironments.org/index.php*) and by the Trace Center.

[4] CAST, the Center for Applied Special Technology, bases its discussion of universal design for learning on the function of these neural networks in individual learners (see excerpt above, and Rose and Meyer, 2002, and CAST's Web site: *http://CAST.org*).

4

ASSISTIVE TECHNOLOGY AND UNIVERSAL DESIGN FOR LEARNING IN CONTENT AREAS

In this chapter, you will learn:

- how UDL and assistive technology can be applied to specific content areas

- examples of UDL and assistive technology being applied to content areas

- how to evaluate technologies and UDL environments

Briarwood: Benefiting all Students

Ms. Woodman, the principal of Ms. Anderson's school, visits a few classrooms during teacher evaluation observations and notes that several teachers are using very specific routines in their classroom that seem to benefit all the students. These UDL strategies include chunking main ideas and working with them across the curriculum so that students learning vocabulary in one area can use it for advanced applications and technologies in math and science. She decides that these ideas should be shared at the next faculty meeting. Four of the teachers prepare a brief presentation, which is well received by the faculty. Ms. Woodman puts together a unique professional development plan that allows teachers to rotate through the classrooms of the four presenters. After the rotations are complete, the four presenters oversee focus groups at each of the next two faculty meetings to answer questions and help colleagues plan for implementation of one of the principles of UDL during second semester. Faculty learning about UDL are interested in student outcomes in the four model classes so the four presenters will collect that data and present at the final faculty meeting of the year.

What UDL strategies have you used or observed in the classroom; and how did those strategies benefit the entire classroom?

ASSISTIVE TECHNOLOGY AND UNIVERSAL DESIGN FOR LEARNING STRATEGIES

Remember that, for some students, assistive technology (AT) is a requirement for instruction because without it they cannot function academically. It is true that the same AT device that is used for one student to function may just be a useful support for another. Realizing this, teachers must consider student requirements through the use of assessments and AT consideration guides available in their school or district. Some of the strategies that emerge from the consideration process may result not only in ways to motivate and engage students in learning but also in options that allow students to rely on their preferred learning paths for engaging with the new information and demonstrating that learning has occurred. Teachers must also be aware that AT falls along a continuum of low to high tech, with low tech including non-technology-based strategies and high tech including the greatest level of technology through the use of a computer or other computer-related device, such as a hand-held mobile electronic tool.

When organizing activities for students, it is useful to explore specific content and to consider how to provide the appropriate learning activities that integrate the use of UDL tools so that the student, with assistance as needed from peers and teachers, masters the material. Teachers must realize also that the ideal learning zone for an individual student is one that is challenging, but not overwhelming, and one that ensures that the information is relatively easy to understand without being simplistic or boring for the student. To assist students in learning the key themes, it is helpful to use conspicuous strategies (teaching students how to approach learning), mediated scaffolding—using supports to introduce skills and concepts and gradually removing those supports when they are no longer needed by students—and ensuring that instruction is tied to background knowledge, i.e., what the student already knows. It is also useful to consider that while an AT device may be a current requirement for a student to function, over time it may become obsolete as students make progress and achieve.

Remember that the key to UDL is the flexibility it affords the teacher and each learner, over time, across content, and with changing technologies available in the marketplace. With UDL, the teacher, who is familiar with the abilities of her class, has a toolbox of instructional methods from which she can produce the right tool for the right job. This same teacher understands where technology strategies are requirements for students to learn. In addition, the student should be actively engaged as much as possible in making decisions about how to approach his/her learning. By being able to introduce flexibility and equitability into the curriculum at any level, however diverse the classroom is, teachers can provide true access to learning so that every student can participate and progress in the general education curriculum.

The above sections detail how to design and adapt instruction. The following section specifically addresses how to use technology in each cognitive area designated in the curriculum and on students' IEP's. These cognitive areas include reading, writing, communication, math, and science. The purpose of these next sections is to review some of the technologies that can be used in different curriculum areas and for different skills. Readers should constantly remind themselves to imagine how different students with disabilities might benefit from greater or lesser structure as it relates to the features identified by the use of specific software programs and instructional strategies.

Applying Assistive Technology in Writing

Writing is a complex task that requires the integration of a number of different skills: the writer must generate basic ideas, organize thoughts to elaborate on these ideas, and then construct sentences and paragraphs to communicate these ideas. Students who experience problems with the mechanics of writing may be poor spellers, have illegible handwriting, or have difficulty composing new text. Some of the tools used to support various aspects of writing are described below.

AT that Supports the Mechanics of Writing

The mechanics of writing include skills such as automatic letter formation, use of space, basic spelling, capitalization and punctuation, speed, clarity of expression, and appropriate grammar. Numerous AT supports are available to students with these difficulties. Low-tech solutions often used include raised lined paper, adding a pencil grip to a traditional pen or pencil, raising the writing surface through the use of a slant board and using ergonomic pens that can provide sensory input and help students become aware of the relationship between the pen and paper.

A variety of software programs has also been developed that provides targeted accommodations to students with disabilities in writing. For example, talking word processors, which speak aloud what is typed into the computer, allow students to use their "general language sense" to monitor their writing (MacArthur, 1999, p. 152). IntelliTalk II (*http://www.intellitools.com*), Write Outloud (*http://www.donjohnston.com*), Type & Talk and Read and Write (*www.texthelp.com*), and eReader (*http://www.cast.org*) are a few examples.

Word prediction software programs, which are used to provide a more efficient means for producing written work and are designed to reduce the number of keystrokes a student types, are appropriate technology for students with fine motor difficulties or problems with vocabulary recall. Word prediction programs have made significant differences in the writing productivity of students with disabilities. These programs "predict" the desired word after a single letter or combination of letters have been typed and offer a menu of word choices from which the student selects the appropriate word (MacArthur, 1998; MacArthur, 1999). The following are examples of word prediction programs: Co:Writer 4000 (*http://www.donjohnston.com*), KeyRep (*http://www.prentrom.com*), Gus Communications (*http://gusinc.com*), and Telepathic 2000 (*http://www.madentec.com*).

Finally, AT, such as speech recognition programs, is available for students with fine motor difficulties or physical disabilities. Higgins and Raskind (2000) found that students using speech recognition tools have demonstrated improvement in their word recognition, reading comprehension, and spelling (Higgins & Raskind, 2000). Dragon Naturally Speaking Preferred (*www.scansoft.com*), iListen 1.5 (*www.macmacspeech.com*) and Abasoft-Talking Listening Desktop Companion (*http://www.talkingdesktop.com*) are examples of speech recognition programs.

Applying Technology that Supports the Composition of Written Thoughts

Many writers struggle with pre-writing tasks such as brainstorming, clustering ideas, and identifying themes or keywords. Frequently, graphic organizers are appropriate ATs to facilitate student success in these activities. Low-tech solutions, such as flow-charting, task analysis, webbing or networking ideas, and outlining strategies, are often used as class-wide strategies while accompanied with targeted high-tech solutions such as Kidspiration (grades K-3) and Inspiration (grades 4 and up) (*www.inspiration.com*) or Draft Builder (*www.donjohnston.com*), which provide the scaffolds for students to learn how to structure and plan their writing assignments.

Students who have limited literacy skills or little prior knowledge in a particular content area may also benefit from visuals and other media for writing (Daiute, 1992). For example, a teacher may give students pictures of farm animals with the corresponding words to prompt their writing about life on the farm. Multimedia writing programs provide teachers with high-tech solutions to address this writing difficulty by providing students with flexible ways to express their thoughts with pictures and sounds. The following multimedia programs are available: Storybook Weaver, the Ultimate Writing and Creativity Center, Student Writing Center (*www.learningcompanyschool.com*), Imagination Express: Destination Series (*http://www.edmark.com*), and Kid Works Deluxe (*www.smartkidssoftware.com/3&4read.htm*).

Note-taking poses another type of challenge for students who have a writing disability because of the fast pace usually associated with classroom lectures. Some low-tech tools provide students with structured outlines with spaces for student-entered information and carbonless notepaper. Portable note-takers such as the Alpha Smart (*www3.alphasmart.com*) and DreamWriter (*www.dreamwriter.com*) are high-tech note-taking devices, which interface directly with the desktop computer and enable students to take notes in settings where they do not have access to a desktop computer.

Applying Assistive Technology to Reading

A competent reader possesses a strong foundation in three primary areas: 1) "alphabetics"—including mastery of the alphabet, understanding the relation of letters and words, knowledge that language is made of words, syllables, and phonemes, and a strong ability to identify letter sounds, sound out new words, and recognize spelling patterns; 2) fluency—defined as "the ability to read connected text rapidly, smoothly, effortlessly, and automatically with little conscious attention to the mechanics of reading, such as decoding" (Meyer & Felton; 1999, p. 284); and 3) an extensive vocabulary (National Reading Panel, 1999).

AT that Supports the Development of Alphabetics

Teachers in the UDL classroom can choose from a variety of tools to increase letter identification, phonics, phonemic awareness, syllable segmentation, and spelling pattern recognition. Simple AT tools such as line drawings, photographs, and picture symbols can be used to teach these skills. While some teachers may develop their own supports, others may use a software programs such as Boardmaker (*www.mayer-johnson.com*), which includes a database of over 3,000 picture symbols that can be formatted, used as flashcards, or used to create adaptive books. Additional AT designed to support emergent readers and those who are struggling with phonics includes Simon Sounds Out (*www.donjohnston.com*), Fast ForWord Basics (*www.scilearn.com*), the Let's Go Read series (*www.riverdeep.net/edmark/*) and Read, Write, & Type (*www.readwritetype.com*).

Instructional and Assistive Technologies that Support Fluency

Repeated readings are frequently used to increase reading fluency. Through the use of AT devices such as taped books, devices that read print books aloud, and talking storybooks, teachers can ensure that students are engaged in repeated reading opportunities without a high level of teacher support. Taped and CD versions of print materials are available through the Reading for the Blind and Dyslexic organization (*www.rfbd.org*) and Living Books (*www.broderbund.com*), which is a series of CD-ROM storybooks that brings popular children's books to life.

Reading fluency, like phonemic awareness and phonics, can also be developed through software programs that target this skill. The Fast ForWord Reading program (*www.scilearn.com*) exercises are designed to be repeated and can be done more than once each day, and Don Johnston's Start-to-Finish Books (*www.donjohnston.com*), which also target fluency, not only give students the benefits of repeated readings, but also have a narrator feature in which the student can hear the book read with careful articulation at an appropriate speed.

AT that Supports Reading Comprehension

Students with strong reading comprehension skills are able to construct meaning from text. Technology is available that allows students who are struggling with decoding and fluency to develop their reading comprehension skills even if they are not yet decoding accurately or reading fluently. For example, the Kurzweil 3000 (*www.kurzweiledu.com*) and *IntelliTools Reading: Story Kits* (*http://www.intellitools.com*) are comprehension programs to support students by reading words aloud, providing decoding assistance, highlighting features that add visual reinforcement, and using songs and folktales to strengthen basic skills and include patterned language, familiar refrains, and vivid graphics.

An on-line resource (*www.readwritethink.org/*) provides a variety of lessons designed to improve reading comprehension skills. For example, one lesson titled *Scaffolding Comprehension Strategies Using Graphic Organizers* is based on the Collaborative Strategic Reading (CSR) approach, which combines reading comprehension strategy instruction and cooperative learning. CSR has not only yielded positive outcomes for students with disabilities but also average and high average achieving students have benefited (Klingner & Vaughn, 1999).

AT that Addresses Risk Factors for Reading Difficulties

Risk factors such as visual, physical, or hearing impairments, inability to concentrate, poor motivation, and lack of access to reading materials can impede a child's reading proficiency. A wide array of ATs that are highly interactive software programs support students with physical and sensory impairments, including auditory output, switch compatible interfaces, and flexibility in on-screen text size. To motivate students, teachers can use productivity software such as Hyperstudio (*www.hyperstudio.com*), IntelliPics Studio (*www.intellitools.com*), and Microsoft Power-Point (*www.microsoft.com*) to create individualized, high-interest books or reading passages. These provide students with reading material that is relevant to their interests, experiences, and background knowledge. Finally, a multimedia web site developed through collaboration among the Western/Pacific LINCS (part of the National Institute for Literacy's LINCS Project), Literacyworks, and CNN's San Francisco bureau provides online literacy opportunities that benefit all learners (literacynet.org/cnnsf/home.html). This site includes comprehensive news stories available in multiple audio and video formats, abridged stories, and story outlines. Low-tech devices available for students with disabilities include materials such as highlighting tape, page-turners, also known as "page fluffers," and reading guides that help students keep their place and focus on the reading passage.

Applying Assistive Technology in Mathematics

Mathematics disabilities are as varied and complex as those associated with reading and can include 1) difficulty processing language, 2) visual spatial confusion, and 3) inability to develop number sense. To master mathematics, children must understand numbers, counting, and the conceptual and procedural features involved in solving simple and complex arithmetic problems (Geary, 1994). Computer-aided instruction and other AT devices that have been shown to be effective tools for teaching mathematics are discussed below.

AT that Supports Processing Language in Math Problems

The language of math poses particular problems for some students, resulting in confusion about terminology, difficulty following verbal explanations and managing the steps of complex calculations, and difficulty attending to teacher explanations or long written practice worksheets. Students with language disorders often require demonstration with concrete materials (Herbert, 1985). ATs such as Blocks in Motion (*www.donjohnston.com*), which allows students to practice problem-solving and critical thinking skills by building patterns, mazes, graphs, buildings, and objects, and IntelliMathics (*www.intellitools.com*), which is a multi-featured tool that uses a variety of on-screen manipulatives such as attribute blocks, geoboards, and base ten blocks to help students solve math problems, provide concrete materials to help students understand the abstract terminology used in math.

AT that Addresses Visual Spatial Confusion

One of the common components of mathematical disabilities is an inability to symbolically or visually represent or code numerical information for storage (Geary, 1990; Geary & Brown, 1991). For example, a student could have difficulty differentiating between numbers (e.g., 6 and 9; 2 and 5; or 17 and 71), coins, operation symbols, and the hands on a clock or difficulty relating to the directional aspects of math such as aligning numbers up-down to do addition and subtraction or left-right for regrouping and reading a number line. Low-tech solutions such as a string abacus, which provides visual and kinesthetic feedback to students, are often used to help these students learn math concepts. High-tech solutions such as Mathpad Plus Fractions and Decimals (*www.intellitools.com*), which is a customizable software program that supports learning of fractions and decimals through the use of pie charts, fraction bars, or decimal grids, are also readily available.

AT that Supports the Development of Number Sense

Number sense is an emerging construct (Berch, 1998) that refers to a child's fluidity and flexibility with numbers, the sense of what numbers mean, and an ability to perform mental mathematics and to look at the world and make comparisons (Gersten & Chard, 1999). Students with difficulties in number sense can benefit from low-tech AT devices such as color-coding columns within a spreadsheet or form. High-tech solutions include programs such as Cruncher 2.0 (*www.knowledgeadventure.com/educators*), which is a program that helps students learn basic spreadsheet functions and can advance to importing and exporting information, adding sounds, and making presentations with graphs they have created on the program. The Graph Club (*www.tomsnyderproductions.com*) supports students in learning how to create and interpret graphs, engages students in mathematical reasoning and problem solving, and links math to their daily lives. Additionally, AT to support students in problem-solving, fractions, number facts, multiplication, and money, such as Edmark Calculator Collection (*www. edmark.com/free/ calculatorcollection.html*), which uses four unique calculators to teach math, is available.

Applying Assistive Technology in Communication

Communication is a process of exchanging information between individuals through a common system of symbols, signs, or behaviors. For some people, this exchange is interrupted or delayed because of a communication disorder, which encompasses a wide variety of problems in language, speech, and hearing. AT can open communication channels through print, symbols, and synthetic speech. AT communication systems are a combination of low-tech to high-tech devices that support the expressive and receptive language needs of the individual student. For those students who have a severe communication disorder, alternative and augmentative communication (AAC) is the method used to achieve functional communication. An AAC device helps a person communicate when traditional spoken or written forms of communication do not meet that person's needs. It may be used instead of speech or in combination with residual natural speech. Several AT devices that support both expressive and receptive communication are discussed below.

AT that Supports Expressive Language

 Students who are nonspeaking or exhibit decreased expressive communication abilities are less likely to have access to and participate in the general curriculum or common activities such as social greetings, making choices, social interaction with peers, and active participation in classroom activities. AT that supports students with decreased expressive communication abilities include low-tech solutions such as picture communication boards, choice boards, alphabet boards, and eye gaze communication boards. Typically these communication boards are created using black line drawings such as the Mayer Johnson Picture Communication Symbols (PCS). Other representations could be real objects, photographs, and simple text.

High-tech solutions such as voice output communication aids (VOCAs), which are electronic devices that generate printed and spoken text, can be combined with the low-tech communication boards to provide voice feedback. VOCAs typically found in the classroom include the Cheap Talk (*www.enablingdevices.com*), the Step by Step Communicator (*www.ablenetinc.com*), the One Step Communicator (*www.ablenetinc.com*), the BigMac (*www.ablenetinc.com*), and the Alpha Talker (*www.prentrom.com*).

Students with severe communication disorders often use dedicated communication devices, which are designed to help students to communicate with others and interact with their environment and are designed solely for augmenting communication. Example devices include the Vanguard (*www.prentrom.com*), the Dynavox (*www.dynavoxsys.com*), or the eTalk (*www.greattalkingbox.com*). Non-dedicated AAC devices include desktop or laptop computers with specialized software. Speaking Dynamically Pro (*www.mayerjohnson.com*), EZ Keys (*http://www.words-plus.com*), and Gus Speech System (*www.gusinc.com*) are examples of communication software packages that transform the computer into a powerful speech-output device.

AT that Supports Receptive Language

Receptive communication is the process of receiving and understanding a message. Behaviors that may indicate problems with receptive language include difficulty remembering instructions or following directions; difficulty with the rate, complexity, or amount of spoken or written information presented at one time; requests for multiple repetition of information; and poor recognition of vocabulary. AT devices can support students who have difficulty understanding language by helping students understand what teachers say, repeating the important points in lectures, and reminding them of assignments and test questions.

Low-tech communication tools use real objects, photographs, or picture symbols to prompt students about their daily schedule at school or at home and provide a visual aid that helps students to understand what needs to be done and when it should be done. Visual schedules help children in the areas of sequencing, organization of time, understanding oral language, and attending. Picture It (Silver Lining Multimedia, Inc.) and Board Maker are two AT software programs that support teachers in creating the picture icons used with these visual aids. Other AT devices help students who have difficulty with the rate, complexity, or amount of spoken or written information presented at a time by permitting the teacher and student to control the rate and amount of information the student is receiving. For example, the Voice-It Plus (*www.recordersplus.com*) is a digital storage device of dictated information and can be used to provide a student with short reminders.

For some students, selecting the right vocabulary to communicate their thoughts can be difficult. Some of the most readily available and simple low-tech tools to help build vocabulary are word-finding games, crossword puzzles, and games like Adlibs. These tools help students learn new words and practice other words they have already acquired.

There are specialized software packages available to assist students who may have more severe communication disorders. The Laureate Company's (*www.llsys.com/*) First Words, First Words II, and First Verbs Sterling Editions train early development of nouns and verbs. These early vocabulary programs help children and adults with special needs master 100 nouns and 50 verbs. *The Words & Concepts Series* teaches vocabulary, categorization, word association, word function, and the concepts of same and different.

EVALUATING ASSISTIVE TECHNOLOGY IN THE CONTENT AREAS

Although the UDL classroom provides a supportive environment for integrating AT, collaborative action plans remain an essential part of the implementation process. AT action plans provide teachers and support personnel with a systematic plan for implementation of the device(s). Components of the plan could include but are not limited to:

1. Describing the instructional activities and settings for which the AT will be used and methods for incorporating AT use into the lessons.
2. Defining when and how the student will be taught to use the AT and determination of who will provide initial and ongoing instruction.
3. Assigning responsibility to persons for maintenance and upgrading of the AT device to ensure it is functioning properly.
4. Designing a system for continuous data collection to monitor and evaluate student progress while using AT.
5. Planning how the student can use the technology in home and community environments.

In the Briarwood case in Chapter 2, the technology action plan designed by Ms. Anderson and the IEP team provided the teachers and support personnel with a strategy for implementing the AT selected for Jorge. The student then received individualized instruction on how to use the programs, the teachers collaborated on how to integrate the use of AT into all classroom writing activities, and data were collected to monitor progress.

Ongoing, curriculum-based monitoring and evaluation of student progress is a key element to creating a successful UDL classroom. The data collected by tracking student progress helps teachers to appropriately modify class-wide strategies to effectively address the needs of all students. Similarly, continuous evaluation of technology is needed. Therefore, it is essential to not only assess whether or not the selected technology provides immediate and adequate support of student needs but also to assess if technology continues to support the student's needs over time. For example, the talking word processor selected for Jorge at the beginning of the year was effective in building Jorge's confidence in completing writing assignments and helping Jorge to organize his thoughts on paper. As the year progressed, Ms. Anderson and the special education teacher tracked Jorge's progress in writing and assessed how effectively the AT was meeting his needs. Using these results, they observed improvement in basic writing skills, but found that Jorge was still not able to complete more complex writing assignments. Thus, the teachers began to research possible AT devices that would meet this specific need.

The benefits to continuous monitoring and evaluating of student progress are apparent throughout all classroom activities. Whether or not the activity is defined by teachers as data collection, teachers collect data every day by administering tests, checking homework, and orally assessing student understanding. By integrating these activities with explicit plans to evaluate and monitor the effectiveness of UDL strategies and AT integration, the teacher will be equipped with the necessary information to ensure that instruction is responsive to the needs of all students in the classroom.

Summary

- AT devices are critical accommodations that help students with disabilities access the instructional activities and materials in the general education classroom. AT provides students with specific learning needs with the necessary targeted support to facilitate their learning so that they are able to successfully achieve alongside with their non-disabled classmates. Even in a well-designed UDL classroom, there may be students whose learning can be further enhanced through the use and implementation of targeted AT devices and services.

- Numerous technology devices are readily available to students and range from low- to high-technology devices. Writing, reading, math, communication, and organization tools were highlighted through this chapter; nevertheless, technology devices and UDL strategies can be used in a multitude of contexts to enhance the lives of individuals with disabilities.

- Selection of a specific device or devices should be based on the individual student's needs, strengths, preferred learning styles, and academic and personal goals.

- IEP team members should develop AT action plans to foster effective implementation of the devices.

- Ongoing monitoring and evaluation of the AT device and its effectiveness in meeting the students' needs based on the task required and supports with the environment are essential.

Questions for Discussion

1. Ms. Woodward, the principal of Briarwood, wants to share teaching strategies with her school. Which strategies would be most important to share for pacing, delivering, and evaluating instruction applicable across content areas?

2. What specific steps would you take to begin developing these strategies?

3. In Chapters 1 and 2, information was provided for considering both AT and UDL. In this chapter, specific examples were provided. From your reading, what specific strategies identified above differentiate AT from UDL?

4. Who can benefit from AT? Is it only intended for students with disabilities?

5. What are specific ways students' learning can be enhanced by AT in the areas of:

   a. Writing?

   b. Reading?

   c. Mathematics?

   d. Communication?

   e. Organization and study skills?

Try This!

1. Research a variety of AT devices that could be used in the UDL classroom. Ensure that the sampling of devices that is discussed ranges in level of technological complexity and proposed function. Explain to students the primary utility, intended population(s), and how to use each device. Discuss the following questions based on your findings

   - What are the intended functions and populations for each device?

   - Are there secondary purposes this device could fulfill? If so, what are they?

   - Would other students benefit from this technology? If so, how?

   - Can you see any potential barriers to the implementation of this technology in the general education classroom? If so, how could these barriers be alleviated?

2. In a small group, develop a scenario in which you believe a student with a disability would benefit from AT. A written description of the scenario should include a description of the classroom setting (i.e., grade, general student characteristics, teaching methodologies employed by teacher, learning opportunities students are currently engaged in, and other pertinent information) and a description of the student (i.e., needs, strengths, preferred learning styles, academic and personal goals). Next, have the groups exchange their scenarios. Each group will determine if targeted AT devices and services should be considered for the student identified in the scenario. If so, what type of assessments should be conducted? What are some potential ATs that could benefit the student? Lastly, groups should briefly present their findings to the whole class.

3. Is AT *necessary* in an appropriately designed UDL classroom?

5

COLLABORATIVE STRATEGIES FOR UNIVERSAL DESIGN FOR LEARNING SUCCESS

In this chapter, you will learn:

- Specific strategies for implementing UDL in different environments

- Strategies to use before, during, and after instruction to consistently modify curriculum based on student needs

- The importance of team building and collaboration

- Requirements for professional development around UDL

Briarwood: Collaborating for Success

Based on a discussion with several teachers struggling with implementing UDL in the classroom, Ms. Anderson decides to visit a few of those teachers classrooms during the school day to provide some suggestions on how they might more effectively integrate UDL principles and AT strategies. While visiting Mr. Parker, a teacher who expressed his frustration, she notices that he has several students in special education working with general education students to complete writing assignments. While Mr. Parker has these students working together, she notices that there is no structure behind the activity and the several students are not participating in their group, sitting quietly in the circle, or completing the activity. In another group, the speech and language pathologist is working one-on-one with a student; but the other children in that group are becoming disruptive. Ms. Anderson suggests that Mr. Parker may want to build into the activity varied ways for all students to participate. He suggests that Ms. Anderson, the speech-language pathologist and he meet to discuss some strategies that were discussed at the professional development inservice around universal design for learning. He would like the speech-language pathologist to align her interventions with the overall instructional methods used in the class. In order to do this, a good deal of coordination is in order. He asks Ms. Anderson how she might help him to coordinate this for the students' benefit. Ms. Anderson notes that the focus of that coordination and collaboration should be on the fundamental design of learning activities in his class as derived from observations of all three professionals about students' learning strengths and weaknesses.

How could you encourage your colleagues in general and special education, as well as the service providers, to meet to discuss the integration of UDL in the classroom?

DESIGNING AND IMPLEMENTING UDL ENVIRONMENTS

Implementing UDL as a regular part of the educational process must include a high degree of collaboration among administration, teachers, and specialists as they focus together on the goal of increasing student understanding and achievement. To build systemic change, implementation must also be practical and personal; the teacher is the one essential component in realizing reform, and effective teaching methods are always key to making permanent changes in the classroom.

Many of the techniques that teachers will use to provide the necessary flexibility for UDL are already in practice to some degree. Techniques such as collaborative teaching and student-centered instruction have resulted partially from legislation mandating inclusion, but their success extends beyond compliance with the law. Teachers who have gifted students in their class, for example, may already be familiar with differentiated instruction. Those who have employed assistive technology to accommodate students with disabilities already may have an understanding of the principles behind UDL. And caring teachers who have students whose primary language is not English know how to use multiple means of presenting a lesson so that it becomes meaningful.

What's new about universal design for learning is how it incorporates a number of best and promising practices in education under one umbrella so that rather than shopping around for a variety of accommodations to meet the needs of several students, teachers will understand the best means of organizing and delivering the instruction. Universally designed curricular materials allow teachers to go to one source for many built-in accommodations, such as physical or cognitive support systems. To understand universal design for learning is to understand how to increase the flexibility of content (curricular materials), process (instructional techniques), and product (student work). To understand UDL is also to understand both how a teacher's instructional flexibility is needed to provide accommodations to students and how technology can facilitate those accommodations. Curricular materials that incorporate the principles of UDL include numerous opportunities for flexibility, with both accommodations and technologies built into the materials themselves. With a UDL curriculum, students have opportunities to determine how they learn (teachers provide multiple ways of presenting the lesson content), how they respond to the materials (teachers allow for multiple means of student engagement), and how they demonstrate their learning (teachers provide multiple means of expression). With UDL technology in place in the classroom, students can press a button on a computer and have instantaneous access to accommodations.

The central, underlying premise behind the concept of UDL is that flexibility is inherent in teaching, learning, and assessment to accommodate all learners. Access to the curriculum can be further facilitated with the integration of technology to ensure that students with disabil-

ities have every opportunity afforded their non-disabled peers to progress in the general education curriculum.

How UDL Impacts Curricular Areas

Thinking of universal design for learning solely as a matter of instructional materials is like thinking of music as just a bunch of instruments. While instruments are critical, there is the melody, rhythm, harmonies, voice, etc. In classrooms, teachers will have opportunities to help students find their own rhythms and create their own melodies and harmonies. Likewise, the group lesson will have its own melody. Teachers have many opportunities to present curriculum content using UDL methodologies. And while UDL materials, like instruments, add richness to classroom resources, UDL materials are not themselves enough for teachers to adopt UDL teaching strategies and approaches. For example, teachers may wish to present lessons that provide students *options* for how they approach learning, for how they interact with curriculum content, and how they display their knowledge.

When teachers present UDL lessons, they provide students with many options. These options provide for flexibility in how complex the material is, how students use their time, how many and what kind of supports are provided to students, and how students are assessed. As teachers find materials that have UDL features, they may be tempted to simply make those materials available to students who can opt to use them. However, such a process could unfortunately result in insufficient use of the UDL materials for the very students for whom this is most important.

Consideration should be given to how to ensure that students with some of the most significant cognitive, sensory, physical, and behavioral disabilities will benefit from the materials. For this to happen, educators will need to consider all they know about effective instructional strategies and employ many of those strategies in teaching students how to use these UDL features. For example, task analysis is invaluable for breaking instruction into the components that are needed to increase proficiency with a task. Some of the other strategies that might be useful for instruction include:

- Demonstrating (modeling) how to use the feature.

- Using cooperative teaching, where students learn together and help each other to understand the task and how to use the materials.

- Ensuring adequate opportunities for practice and mastery.

- Incorporating strategies for generalizing skills so that information learned in one setting or with one type of material can be applied in other settings or with other materials.

- Considering the use of prompting in response to student questions (rather than simply providing answers).

- Establishing a way to instruct that reduces errors and increases speed of performance. (If a technology is too cumbersome, it will stand in the way of efficient use.)

The above strategies have been applied to a wide array of teaching situations and certainly have been used to introduce assistive technologies to learners. They can also be very useful in teaching students through UDL.

STRATEGIES AND INSTRUCTION

While the goal of software publishers and researchers is to have UDL features built into curricular materials, until those features are built in, *teachers can be more effective by intentionally incorporating UDL features into the materials and lessons that they present to students.*

The next section of this chapter briefly identifies a number of classroom practices that will benefit teachers as they move from traditionally designed, textbook-centered methods into more flexible methods that incorporate the principles of universal design for learning into regular practice. As noted above, many of these best practices have already been in place in many classrooms for years. No one instructional method can work in all situations, since the goal is to individualize teaching to that extent that it reaches the most students in the most effective ways. An informed teacher will better know, through learning and through experience, what instructional strategies and methods to apply in a given situation that these general overviews could suggest.

SETTING LEARNING GOALS IN AN INCLUSIVE CLASSROOM

Universal design for learning is more than the use of digital materials or of textbooks that have been adapted to accommodate students with disabilities. If the teacher does not set goals based on the specific needs of her class or employ organized strategies to reach students who may need additional support to understand the lesson, the best computer program or textbook will be no more than a novelty item and the adaptations will cost time and yield few positive results.

One of the best frameworks for illustrating how a teacher can structure teaching was developed by Schumm, Vaughn, and Leavell (1994) and is known as the Planning Pyramid (see Figure 5.1).

This pyramid allows a teacher to organize her approach to each lesson so that she understands the different levels of what to expect in terms of what her class will learn. The bottom level of the pyramid represents material the teacher expects *all* students to learn; this will be the essential concept of the lesson, the "Big Idea," which, when learned, will allow students to progress to the next lesson or level of learning. The next level, somewhat smaller, represents what most but not all students will learn; this indicates the group that the teacher expects to apply more developed or broader skills to gain more in-depth knowledge. The top level of the pyramid represents what some students will learn; students who excel in certain areas of learning will be given educational challenges appropriate to their skills. This information will be more complex and contain a greater number of facts, and the learning will proceed at a faster pace.

The axes of the pyramid represent the five interrelated areas teachers need to consider when planning lessons: student, teacher, topic, context, and instructional practice. The teacher, in strategizing a lesson, will ask herself questions about the abilities of her students, her own preferences for the subject, and what instructional practices she could employ; she will ask questions about the complexity of the topic and where the topic occurs in regard to previously learned material, and she will ask questions about the classroom context in which the lesson will occur.

This approach toward lesson planning fosters a differentiated curriculum. To use the pyramid's strategies successfully, a teacher must know the range of abilities of the students in her class and plan for success for each of them. Although all students will be taught the same lesson, not all students will be taught the same number of facts at the same level of complexity or at the same pace. It's important to understand as a teacher employs strategies based on the

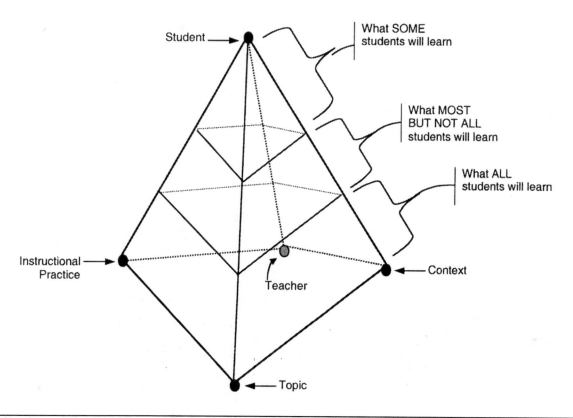

Figure 5.1: The Learning Pyramid for Instructional Planning. *Source: Original pyramid from Schumm, Vaughn, & Leavell (1994). Using the pyramid to structure lessons for diverse learners in Schumm (1999), http://www.ed.gov/pubs/ModStrat/*

pyramid that the three "levels" are not meant to track students, "dumb down" the lessons, or lower expectations of what anyone can achieve. The pyramid helps a teacher strategize the larger issues of content and delivery and to understand where to individualize instruction. Careful use of this pyramid will help ensure that all students master some of the content for the lesson, and that the focus for those students who have difficulty learning will be on the most essential content—the big ideas.

PROFESSIONAL DEVELOPMENT AND COLLABORATION

McLaughlin (2002) recommends some ways to better prepare teachers and schools to meet the needs of students with exceptionalities, including:

- professional development activities that orient special education teachers to the general curriculum and facilitate their understanding of that curriculum,

- more strategic interaction between general and special educators about the larger curriculum, and

- development of strong professional communities within schools.

Underlying each of the reforms proposed by McLaughlin is the need for better, outcome-based communication among general and special educators. Moreover, implementing the first reform—joint professional development activities—can set the stage for more strategic inter-actions, and it is only after a period of such interactions that strong collaborative professional communities that are inclusive of general and special educators emerge. Such communities, while essential to joint implementation of general education curriculum with *all* students, can-not be forced, but rather are created because of their perceived value by the participants. And that value can only be understood if the dialogue between special and general educators allows both to understand each other's relationship to the general curriculum.

While the reform measures noted above are necessary for creating an atmosphere in which universal design for learning will flourish, they should not necessarily be seen as defining a UDL classroom, just as the access provided by the measures described in Figure 5.2 cannot guarantee but do foster schools where UDL can be more easily implemented.

While an inflexible, one-size-fits-all curriculum might work in a classroom where all chil-dren have the same abilities and style of learning, today a typical classroom now includes many students with cultural and linguistic differences, and students who are at-risk or have disabilities and other special needs. Teachers need to develop flexible teaching strategies in flexible environments to help them reach the greatest number of students.

UDL provides a timely opportunity for general and special educators as well as service providers to interact and collaborate on decision-making for all students—and create the pro-fessional communities advocated by McLaughlin (2002), as it can serve as a catalyst for dis-cussion among general and special educators about how their common concerns can be implemented into the curriculum. However, the nature of collaborative planning needs to shift

---

Successful student access to the general education curriculum is most likely when there is general acceptance of the following principles:

Teachers Use Collaborative Practices

• Unproductive traditions and beliefs are abandoned and replaced with validated practices and a full under-standing of the intent of the law.

• The general education teacher and the special education teacher share responsibility for the learning out-comes of special education students.

• Both understand each student's abilities and needs and both play a significant role in determining IEP goals and providing instruction to help the student reach them.

• Time is allocated for teachers to collaborate with other teachers and parents regarding students. (Ideally, paid days at the end of each school year are provided so that teachers can discuss their students, improving the students' chances for smooth transitions to the next grade.)

The School Functions as a Team

• Administrators understand that teachers need time within their contracts to prepare standards-based activities and materials designed to meet the diverse needs of their students.

• Parents are considered to be part of the team.

Instruction Is Flexible, Expectations Are High

• Expectations are not set according to a student's classification; a classification does not determine how much or how well the student will learn or perform.

• It is understood that good instruction incorporates variation in delivery, activities, expectations, and assess-ment to accommodate diverse learning strengths and needs.

• Accountability is considered a challenge, not a threat. As required by IDEA '97, students with disabilities are included in state and district assessments.

Figure 5.2: Successful Student Access to the General Curriculum. *Source: adapted from the ERIC digest,* Access to the General Education Curriculum for Students with Disabilities, *Beckman,* http://ericec.org/digests/e615.html

to focus on planning over the longer term, i.e., across grade levels, and identifying the critical content, knowledge, and skills that every student must master. Strategic decisions need to be made about how to use scarce instructional time and which skills, concepts, and constructs to teach. Most schools have teacher curriculum committees and many schools offer opportunities for some teachers to engage in curriculum planning, often over the summer break. These are two excellent forums for empowering general and special educators and other educational providers to work together on the implementation of UDL in their schools.

Summary

- The central underlying concept of UDL is that flexibility is inherent in teaching, learning, and assessing to accommodate all learners.

- By differentiating curriculum and instruction, teachers can structure their teaching by organizing each lesson to ensure all students learn.

- Educators should collaborate for a successful UDL environment. Team building and collaboration methods are essential to successful universal designed classrooms and should be fundamental in professional development planning.

Questions for Discussion

- Discuss barriers to curriculum access for students in the classes you teach or plan to teach.

- In the Briarwood example, what specific issues would you make sure Mr. Parker discussed with the speech-language pathologist?

- How should Mr. Parker structure the collaboration activity so that all students could participate?

- What specific professional development content would you recommend to help Mr. Parker with his current classroom situation?

- In general, what role does collaboration play in helping individuals with different instructional paradigms become more cohesive?

Try This!

1. On the Internet, search for a Web site that has curricular materials about universal design for learning. At that site find examples that support the use of UDL for each of the following:
   - Increasing the choices students have about how material is presented
   - Increasing the choices students have about how they engage with materials
   - Increasing the choices students have about how they demonstrate their understanding of the material
   - Providing for built-in accommodations
   - Providing for digital text with built-in adaptations

2. Using the issues identified in this chapter, discuss how collaboration could enhance a teacher's ability to integrate UDL in the classroom.

3. Answer the question proposed by Mr. Parker in the Briarwood example. What are the differences between UDL and traditional curricula; how much time is necessary to create adapted instruction; what supports are necessary to deal with the instructional theories presented in this book?

Conclusion

As the general education classroom becomes, increasingly, the environment in which students with disabilities receive their special education services, application of universal design for learning principles increases the chance for all students to learn and demonstrate what they know. As classroom structures and program designs become the responsibility of all professionals providing instruction and support, establishing a UDL foundation, supplemented by appropriate assistive and other instructional technologies, allows for seamless delivery of all academic and related supports. Through a collaborative team effort that recognizes the unique learning styles of all students, the important outcomes students strive for can be attained.

BIBLIOGRAPHY

Adaptive Environments. *http://www.adaptenv.org/*.

American Federation of Teachers. (2001). *Making standards matter 2001: An annual fifty-state report of efforts to raise academic standards.* Washington, DC: Author.

Agran, M., Snow, K., & Swaner, J. (1999). A survey of secondary level teachers' opinions on community-based instruction and inclusive education. *Journal of the Association for Persons with Severe Handicaps, 24,* 58–62.

Bechard, S. (2000, October). Students with disabilities and standards-based reform, McREL Policy Brief. Mid-continent Research for Education and Learning Laboratory, Denver, CO.

Berch, D.B. (Ed.). (1998, April). *Mathematical cognition: From numerical thinking to mathematics education.* Conference presented by the National Institute of Child Health and Human Development. Bethesda, MD.

Bowser, G., & Reed, P. (1998). Navigating the process: Educational tech points for parents. *Exceptional Parent, 28* (11), 28–31.

Caine, R., & Caine, G. (1997). *Education on the edge of possibility.* Association for Supervision and Curriculum Development, Alexandria, VA.

Caine, R., & Caine, G. (1991). *Making connections: Teaching and the human brain.* (rev. 1994). New York: Pearson Learning.

Cavanaugh, T. (2001). *The need for assistive technology in educational technology.* Retrieved July 5, 2002, from *www.aace.org/pubs/etr/issue2/cavanaugh.cfm*.

Center for Applied Special Technology. (2002). "The Learning Brain" (*http://www.cast.org/udl/TheLearning-Brain10.cfm?*). Retrieved July 15, 2002, from *http://www.cast.org*.

Center for Universal Design, North Carolina State University. (2002). Retrieved August 12, 2004, from *http://www.design.ncsu.edu/cud/*.

Children with Communication Disorders. (1990). ERIC Digest #E470. Retrieved April 18, 2003, from *http://www.ericae.net/edo/ED321504.htm*.

Civil Rights Act of 1964, Pub. L. No. 88-352, 78 Stat. 225.

Daiute, C. (1992). Multimedia composing: Extending the resources of kindergarten to writers across the grades. *Language Arts, 69,* 250–260.

Eichinger, J., & Downing, J.E. (2002). Instruction in the general education environment. In J. Downing (Ed.), *Including students with severe and multiple disabilities in typical classrooms: Practical strategies for teachers (2nd ed.).* Baltimore: Paul H. Brookes Publishing Company.

Gardner, H. (1983). *Frames of mind: The theory of multiple intelligences.* New York: Basic Books.

Gardner, H. (2000). *Intelligence reframed: Multiple intelligences for the 21st century.* New York: Basic Books.

Genesee, Fred. (2000). *Brain research: Implication for second language learning.* ERIC Clearinghouse on Languages and Linguistics, December 2000, ERIC Digest #EDO-FL-00-12; *http://www.cal.org/ericcll/digest/0012brain.html*

Geary, D.C. (1990). A componential analysis of an early learning deficit in mathematics. *Journal of Experimental Child Psychology, 49* (3), 363–383.

Geary, D.C. (1994). *Children's mathematical development: Research and practical applications.* Washington, DC: American Psychological Association.

Geary, D.C., & Brown. S.C. (1991). Cognitive addition: Strategy choice and speed-of-processing differences in gifted, normal, and mathematically disabled children. *Developmental Psychology, 27* (3), 398–406.

Gent, P., & Gurecka, L. (1998). Service learning. A creative strategy for inclusive classrooms. *Journal of the Association for Persons with Severe Handicaps, 23,* 261–271.

Gersten, R., & Chard, D. (1999). Number sense: Rethinking arithmetic instruction for students with mathematical disabilities. *The Journal of Special Education, 44,*18–28.

Gifford, B., & Enyedy, N. (1999) *Activity-centered design: Towards a theoretical framework of CSCL.* Paper presented at the 1999 CSCS99 International Conference on Computer Supported Collaborative Learning. Stanford, CA.

Herbert, E. (1985). One point of view: Manipulatives are good mathematics. *Arithmetic Teacher, 32* (4).

Higgins, E.L., & Raskind, M.H. (2000). Speaking to read: The effects of continuous vs. discrete recognition systems on the reading and spelling of children with learning disabilities. *Journal of Educational Technology, 15* (1), 19–30.

Hitchcock, C., Meyer, A.M., Rose, D., & Jackson, J. (2002). *Access to, participation, and progress in the general curriculum.* (Technical Brief). Peabody, MA: National Center on Accessing the General Curriculum.

Hutchins, E. (1995). *Cognition in the wild.* Cambridge, MA: MIT Press.

Individuals with Disabilities Education Act Amendments of 1997, Pub. L. No. 105-17, 20 U.S.C. 1400 et seq. (1997).

Jones, M.M., & Carlier, L.L. (1995). Creating inclusionary opportunities for learners with multiple disabilities: A team-teaching approach. *TEACHING Exceptional Children, 27,* 23–27.

Kauffman, D., Johnson, S.M., Kardos, S.M., Liu, E., & Peske, H.G. (2002). Lost at sea: Without a curriculum, navigating instruction can be tough—especially for new teachers. *American Educator* (Summer), *47,* 10–26.

Klingner, J.K., & Vaughn, S. (1999). Promoting reading comprehension, content learning, and English acquisition through collaborative strategic reading (CSR). *The Reading Teacher, 52,* 738–747.

Kluth, P. (2000). Community-referenced learning and the inclusive classroom. *Remedial and Special Education, 21,* 19–26.

MacArthur, C. (1998). From illegible to understandable: How word prediction and speech synthesis can help. *TEACHING Exceptional Children, 30* (6), 66–71.

MacArthur, C. (1999). Overcoming barriers to writing: Computer support for basic writing skills. *Reading & Writing Quarterly: Overcoming Learning Difficulties, 15* (2), 169–192.

McLaughlin, M.J. (2002). *Access to the general education curriculum: Paperwork and procedures for redefining special education.* Retrieved from *http://www.casecec.org/pdf/documents/Access_to_the_General_Education_Curriculum.pdf.*

Meyer, M., & Felton, R. (1999). Repeated reading to enhance fluency: Old approaches and new directions. *Annals of Dyslexia, 49,* 283–306.

Meyer, A., & Rose, D. (2002). *Teaching every student in the digital age: Universal design for learning.* Association for Supervision and Curriculum Development. Alexandria, VA.

No Child Left Behind Act of 2001, Pub. L. No. 107–110, 115 Stat. 1425 (2002). Sec. 1111 (b).

Okolo, C.M., Bahr, C.M., & Reith, H.J. (1993). A retrospective view of computer-based instruction. *Journal of Special Education Technology, 12* (1), 1–27.

Pellegrino. J.W., & Goldman. S. R. (1987). Information processing and elementary mathematics. *Journal of Learning Disabilities, 20*(57), 23–32.

Schukar, R. (1997). Enhancing the middle school curriculum through service learning. *Theory into Practice, 36,* 176–183.

Schumm, J.S., Vaughn, S., & Leavell, A. (1994). Pyramid planning: A framework for planning for diverse students' needs during content area instruction. *The Reading Teacher, 47*(8), 608–615.

Temple, E., Deutsch, G.K., Poldrack, R.A., Miller, S.L., Tallal, P., Merzenich, M.M, & Gabrieli, J.D.E. (2003). Neural deficits in children with dyslexia ameliorated by behavioral remediation: Evidence from functional MRI. *Proceedings of the National Academy of Science, USA, 100,* 2860–2865.

US Department of Education, Office of Special Education Programs. (2001, July). *Proceedings of the Capacity Building Institute on access, participation, and progress in the general K-12 curriculum. Appendix B: The comprehensive planning process for the IDEA Part D national program.* 26. *http://www.ncset.org/institutes/proceedings/2002_07_2.pdf.*

Vygotsky, L.S. (1978). *Mind in society: The development of higher order psychological processes.* Cambridge, MA: Harvard University Press.

Wisconsin Literacy Education and Reading Network Source. (n.d.). *Struggling Readers.* Retrieved April 18, 2003, from *http://wilearns.state.wi.us/apps/.*

INDEX